SUMMER STUDY

GRADE
5

FlashKids

New York

New York

An Imprint of Sterling Publishing
1166 Avenue of the Americas
New York, NY 10036

ISBN 978-1-4114-7861-9

Distributed in Canada by Sterling Publishing Co., Inc.
c/o Canadian Manda Group, 664 Annette Street
Toronto, Ontario, Canada M6S 2C8
Distributed in the United Kingdom by GMC Distribution Services
Castle Place, 166 High Street, Lewes, East Sussex, England BN7 1XU
Distributed in Australia by Capricorn Link (Australia) Pty. Ltd.
P.O. Box 704, Windsor, NSW 2756, Australia

For information about custom editions, special sales, and premium and corporate purchases, please contact Sterling Special Sales at 800-805-5489 or specialsales@sterlingpublishing.com.

Manufactured in Canada
Lot #:
2 4 6 8 10 9 7 5 3 1
03/16

www.flashkids.com

Dear Parent,

As a parent, you want your child to have time to relax and have fun during the summer, but you don't want your child's math and reading skills to get rusty. How do you make time for summer fun and also ensure that your child will be ready for the next school year?

This Summer Study workbook provides short, fun activities to help children keep their skills fresh all summer long. This book not only reviews what children learned during fourth grade, it also introduces what they'll be learning in fifth grade. Best of all, the games, puzzles, and stories help children retain their knowledge as well as build new skills. By the time your child finishes the book, he or she will be ready for a smooth transition into fifth grade.

As your child completes the activities in this book, shower him or her with encouragement and praise. You can feel good knowing that you are taking an active and important role in your child's education. Helping your child complete the activities in this book is providing an excellent example—that you value learning every day! Have a wonderful summer, and most of all, have fun learning together!

Preposition Poem

A **preposition** is a word that indicates direction, time, and location of nouns and pronouns. Read this preposition poem. Underline the prepositions. The first one is done for you.

Out the door,
Down the street,
Around the corner,
Onto the bus,
Into my seat,
Off the bus,
Over the playground,
Into my classroom,
School!

Now, write your own preposition poem! Choose a topic that includes lots of action, like playing a sport or making a meal. The last line should summarize or tell the topic. Use as many different prepositions as you can. Use the words in the box to help you.

about	above	across	after	around	at	before
below	beside	by	down	during	for	from
inside	into	of	off	on	out	outside
over	through	to	under	up	with	without

My mom read over 50 books. She would take books outside and inside. She would read the same books about 3 times. She would always from the end to remember what happend during the story. Here she goes again, reading into another book

Ralph's Rotten Day

Read the story and fill in the chart to show the cause and effect.

It all started when Ralph's alarm clock didn't go off in the morning. He woke up late and didn't have time for breakfast. Ralph ran out the door, and he kept running all the way to school. In fact, he ran so fast that he tripped and fell down! Ralph made it to school just as the bell rang.

Ralph's teacher, Mr. Grundy, asked the students to hand in their homework. Ralph had forgotten his homework, so he was the last person to be dismissed for lunch. "At least I didn't forget my lunch," Ralph thought.

At lunchtime, Ralph sat at the lunch tables with his friends and ate his sandwich. Maybe his rotten day was over. As he stood up from the table, he noticed something sticky on his pants. Ralph had sat on bubble gum! For the rest of the day, every time Ralph sat down, he stuck to the chair.

"Let's hope your rotten luck doesn't stick around much longer!" Mr. Grundy joked.

CAUSE	EFFECT
The alarm clock didn't go off.	1. Ralph woke up late and didn't have time for breakfast.
Ralph ran to school very fast.	2.
3.	Ralph was the last person dismissed for lunch.
4.	Every time Ralph sat down, he stuck to the chair.

Sunny Sums

Add or subtract the numbers.

1. 3452
    − 1435
    ‾‾‾‾
    2017

2. 3177
    + 2354
    ‾‾‾‾

3. 5041
    − 3405
    ‾‾‾‾

4. 1989
    + 4036
    ‾‾‾‾

5. 7432
    − 5219
    ‾‾‾‾

6. 4820
    + 2129
    ‾‾‾‾

7. 6271
    − 2480
    ‾‾‾‾

8. 2364
    + 3478
    ‾‾‾‾

9. 8710
    − 1842
    ‾‾‾‾

10. 4836
    + 3719
    ‾‾‾‾

11. 4321
    3210
    + 356
    ‾‾‾‾

12. 2645
    1082
    + 226
    ‾‾‾‾

13. 1573
    1827
    + 4451
    ‾‾‾‾

14. 3509
    4055
    + 1021
    ‾‾‾‾

Rounding Up, Rounding Down

Rounding numbers is easy! Here's how you do it.

> **Example:** Round 45,320 to the nearest hundred.
> - Look at the number to the right of the hundreds place. It is a 2.
> - If the number is 5 or greater, round up.
> - If the number is 4 or less, round down.
>
> **Answer:** 45,300

Round these numbers. Then go back to your answers. Circle the number asked for in the answer. For example, if you are rounding to the nearest hundred, circle the number in the hundreds place. The first one is done for you.

1. 3,288 to the nearest ten

_____3,2⑨0_____ W

2. 8,663 to the nearest ten

_____ L

3. 17,415 to the nearest hundred

_____ A

4. 92,677 to the nearest thousand

_____ C

5. 211,661 to the nearest thousand

_____ S

6. 105,013 to the nearest ten thousand

_____ M

7. 25,538 to the nearest ten

_____ A

8. 855,449 to the nearest ten thousand

_____ Y

9. 66,752 to the nearest hundred

_____ R

10. 19,420 to the nearest thousand

_____ T

11. 500,242 to the nearest hundred

_____ E

12. 678,935 to the nearest ten thousand

_____ D

13. 35,743 to the nearest ten

_____ A

14. 70,518 to the nearest thousand

_____ O

To solve the riddle, find the letters next to the circled even numbers and write them below. Unscramble the letters and write the answer to the riddle on the lines.

Riddle: Where can you buy a ruler that is three feet long?

Answer: ____ ____ ____ ____ ____ ____ ____ ____ ____

Hink Pinks

Read the clues to complete the hink pinks or hinky pinkies.
Add an adjective or a noun.

Hink pinks are one-syllable words that rhyme. The first word is usually an adjective, and the second word is usually a noun.
What is a squashed kitty? *Flat cat*

Hinky pinkies are two-syllable words that rhyme.
What is a rabbit with a sense of humor? *Funny bunny*

Clue	Adjective	Noun
1. Cooked reptile	baked	snake
2. Tidy road		street
3. Plastic pond	fake	
4. Sad footwear		shoe
5. Cat in love	smitten	
6. Happy father	glad	
7. Spicy place		spot
8. Large swine	big	
9. Tired flower	lazy	
10. Fruit needing a shave		berry
11. Bad attitude	rude	
12. Drenched animal		pet
13. Tiny sphere		ball
14. "Hip" monster		ghoul
15. Lawful bird	legal	

Who's the Boss?

Read about the three levels of government. Then write some notes in the space below about what each level does.

No matter where you live in the United States, you have three groups of leaders looking out for you. Your **local** neighborhood is part of a city or town. People in your town elect a mayor as a leader. Each city has a school district to oversee the schools in its area. Cities and towns are grouped into a larger area called a county. Your city or county provides police officers and firefighters to protect the people.

You are also a citizen of the **state** where you live. The governor is the head of a state and has lots of people to help him or her. In fact, each state has three branches of government: executive, legislative, and judicial. Each state also has its own constitution. State governments can give out licenses like drivers' licenses. They have to oversee businesses within the state as well.

All the states belong to the **federal** government. The federal government also has executive, legislative, and judicial branches of government. These three branches are explained in the US Constitution. The federal government has a lot of responsibilities. It prints money and oversees the post office. It also provides armed forces to protect our country. Only the federal government can declare war or make a treaty with another country. The president is the head of the executive branch.

Whether it's local, state, or federal government, they all have the same main purpose. They look out for the well-being of the citizens!

Local

State

Federal

Counting Cash

Look at each money value shown in the chart. Use the least amount of bills and coins to make that value. Then answer the questions below.

Value	$5 bill	$1 bill	quarter	dime	nickel	penny
$3.52	0	3	2	0	0	2
$6.23						
$4.78						
$8.92						
$7.03						
$5.16						
$9.44						
$2.65						
$8.90						
$4.86						
$3.99						
$9.67						

Answer each question. Write the least number of bills and coins received.

1. Josh's lunch was $7.27. He paid with two $5 bills. How much change did he get back? _____

   $1 bills _____ quarters _____ dimes _____ nickels _____ pennies _____

2. Anya bought trail mix and juice for $2.85. She paid with a $5 bill. How much change did she get back? _____

   $1 bills _____ quarters _____ dimes _____ nickels _____ pennies _____

A Very Loud Day

How many things would it take to make a very loud day?
Write the plural for each noun to find out.

1. 1 howling wolf   6 howling   _wolves_

2. 1 crying baby   2 crying   _____

3. 1 honking horn   4 honking   _____

4. 1 tumbling box   10 tumbling   _____

5. 1 yelling man   5 yelling   _____

6. 1 buzzing fly   3 buzzing   _____

7. 1 squeaking mouse   7 squeaking   _____

8. 1 marching band   5 marching   _____

9. 1 giggling elf   10 giggling   _____

10. 1 ticking watch   20 ticking   _____

11. 1 screeching monkey   14 screeching   _____

12. 1 crashing car   12 crashing   _____

13. 1 breaking glass   8 breaking   _____

14. 1 bleating sheep   25 bleating   _____

15. 1 squealing child   40 squealing   _____

It's a Jungle out There!

Follow the directions below.

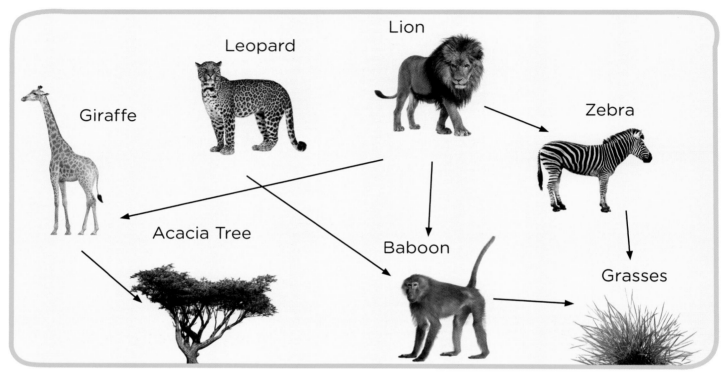

List some of the food chains that are part of this web.

1. ___Acia Tree___   ___Giraffe___   ___Lion___
2. _____   _____   _____
3. _____   _____   _____

For each pair of animals, figure out which one is the predator
and which is the prey. Label each animal.

4. Leopard   Baboon   **5.** Giraffe   Lion

_____   _____   _____   _____

6. Lion   Zebra

_____   _____

Use the food web to complete the lists.

7. Herbivores, or animals that eat plants: **8. Carnivores**, or animals that eat meat:

_____   _____

_____   _____

_____

Raining Cats and Dogs

Follow the directions below.

Have you ever heard the expression, "It's raining cats and dogs"? This is an example of an idiom. The expression means something different from what the words usually mean. This phrase just means that it's raining very hard, not that cats and dogs are falling from the sky!

Draw a line to match each idiom with its meaning.

1. Once in a blue moon
2. Hit the nail on the head
3. Learn the ropes
4. Stick out your neck
5. A piece of cake
6. On cloud nine
7. Through thick and thin
8. Let the cat out of the bag

a) through good times and bad times
b) to give away a secret or surprise
c) once in a while
d) very easy
e) to learn the basics
f) to get something exactly right
g) to go out of your way or take a risk
h) very happy

3 x 3 Magic Squares

All rows and columns in these "magic" squares add up to the magic number. Can you complete the magic squares? Hint: You can use a number only once!

1. All rows and columns add up to 14.

11		
3	7	
		9

2. All rows and columns add up to 16.

	2	
1		
	8	3

3. All rows and columns add up to 20.

10		
8		3
	5	

4. All rows and columns add up to 23.

		2
	12	5
	4	

5. All rows and columns add up to 32.

12		7
17		
		20

6. All rows and columns add up to 45.

	15	
		18
22	16	

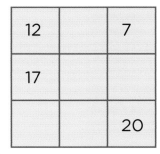

Which Word?

Homophones are words that sound the same
but have different meanings and spellings.

Read the clues for each set of words. One of the words is in the word box. Write it next to the correct clue. Then write the homophones for the other clues.

fowl	flour	its	heel
meet	so	to	whether
do	wood	there	marry

1. Beef _____ *meat* _____
Get to know _____ *meet* _____

2. That place _____
They are _____
Belongs to them _____

3. Bird _____
Not fair _____

4. Milled grain _____
Bloom _____

5. Join together _____
Cheery _____

6. Belonging to it _____
It is _____

7. In order that _____
Mend _____
To plant _____

8. If _____
Condition of air, temperature _____

9. Trunk of a tree _____
Willing to _____

10. Toward a place _____
Also _____
One plus one _____

11. Shall _____
Moisture _____
Owed _____

12. Bottom of foot _____
Make well _____
He will _____

The Gebeta Board: An Ethiopian Folktale

A man carved a beautiful game board, called a gebeta board, out of wood and gave it to his son. The boy loved playing games with the gebeta board and took it everywhere with him.

One day, he came upon a group of men who had no wood to start a fire. The boy gave them his gebeta board to use for firewood. The gebeta board went up in flames, so the men gave him a new knife in its place.

Next, the boy came upon a man digging a well. The boy gave him his new knife to dig with. The ground was so hard that the knife broke. So, the man gave the boy a new spear to take its place.

The boy continued on and met a group of hunters. The hunters used the boy's spear to kill a lion. The spear cracked, so the hunters gave the boy a new horse in its place.

The boy and horse met a group of men working on the road. The workmen made so much noise, the horse got frightened and ran away. The workmen gave the boy an ax in place of the horse.

The boy took the ax and walked toward his village. He lent his new ax to a woodcutter. The woodcutter broke the ax, but he gave the boy a limb of the tree.

The boy carried the limb back to the village. He gave the tree limb to a woman who needed wood for her fire. As the wood went up in flames, the boy began to cry. So, the woman gave him a gebeta board in its place.

When the boy got home, his father smiled and said, "What is better than a gebeta board to keep a boy out of trouble?"

A group of men used the board for firewood and gave the boy a ____knife____ in its place.
1.

When the knife broke, a man gave the boy a _____ in its place.
2.

When the _____ broke, the hunters gave the boy a _____ in its place.
3.   4.

When the _____ ran away, the workmen gave the boy an _____ in its place.
5.   6.

When the _____ broke, a woodcutter gave the boy a _____ in its place.
7.   8.

Round-the-Clock Round Off

Look at the number in the center of each circle. Follow each arrow and round the numbers to the nearest hundred, thousand, ten thousand, and hundred thousand.

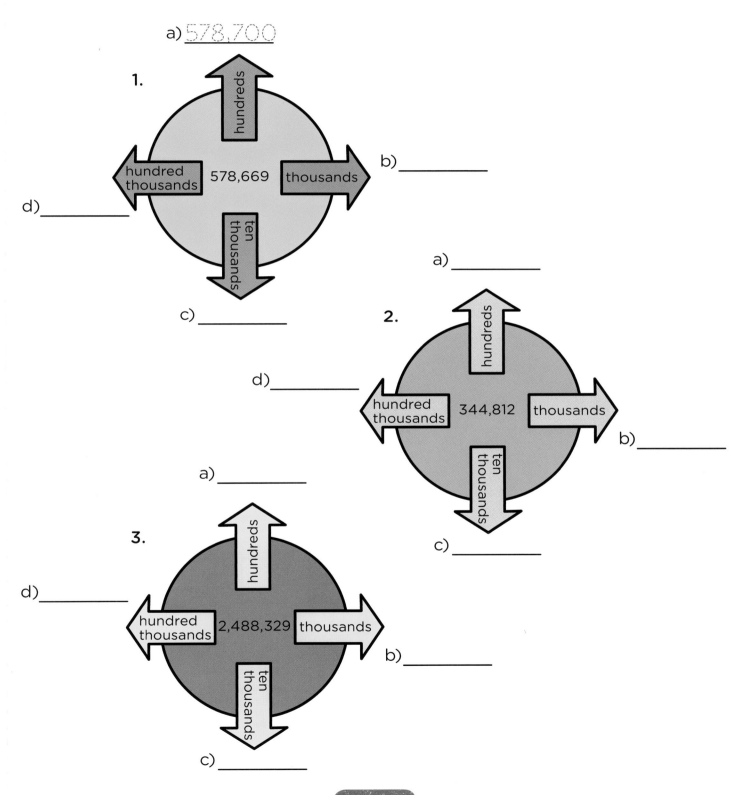

1.

a) 578,700

hundreds

hundred thousands   578,669   thousands

ten thousands

b) _____

d) _____

c) _____

2.

a) _____

hundreds

hundred thousands   344,812   thousands

ten thousands

d) _____

b) _____

c) _____

3.

a) _____

hundreds

hundred thousands   2,488,329   thousands

ten thousands

d) _____

b) _____

c) _____

Practice with Fractions

Follow the directions below.

Rewrite each fraction using numerals.

1. Six and seven-tenths. _____ $6\frac{7}{10}$ _____

2. Fourteen and two-thirds. _____

3. Nine and one-fifth. _____

4. Seventeen and eight-ninths. _____

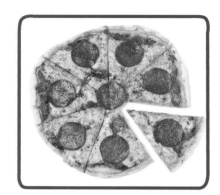

Reduce each fraction.

5. $\frac{17}{4}$ = _____

6. $3\frac{21}{7}$ = _____

7. $8\frac{13}{10}$ = _____

8. $\frac{25}{5}$ = _____

9. $15\frac{10}{3}$ = _____

10. $4\frac{18}{4}$ = _____

Complete each number sentence using >, <, or =.

11. $6\frac{4}{5}$ ☐ $\frac{37}{6}$

12. $\frac{25}{5}$ ☐ $\frac{19}{4}$

13. $\frac{34}{8}$ ☐ $4\frac{1}{2}$

14. $\frac{18}{6}$ ☐ $\frac{12}{4}$

15. $7\frac{9}{3}$ ☐ $8\frac{12}{6}$

16. 5 ☐ $\frac{32}{7}$

Parts of Speech

Identify the parts of speech in each sentence:
noun, adjective, verb, preposition, and article.

Write **N** above the nouns, **ADJ** above the adjectives, **V** above the verbs, **P** above the prepositions, and **A** above the articles.

> ADJ   N   V A ADJ   N P A N
> **Example:** Merry Mario made a mighty mess in the mud.

ADJ N   V   A ADJ N   V   V

1. Wild Willy watched the wavy worms wiggle and wobble.

2. Pretty Patty picked a pricey pink dress.

3. Oliver opened the oven to check on oily omelets.

4. Cheery Charlie chose chunky cheese to chew.

5. Harry the hippo helped Hanna hide huge holey hats.

6. Funny Frannie found flat flowers under the floor.

7. Bored Benny bought bundles of bright blue balloons.

8. Jessica Jones juggled jars of juicy jiggling jelly.

9. Crazy cats crooned and cried under the moon.

10. Dizzy Darryl drove his dusty dog in his dirty truck.

11. Lumpy, lounging lions laughed and licked lollipops.

12. A team of tired tigers tasted ten tangy tacos for a treat.

Nuts about Numbers

Follow the directions below.

Write each set of numbers in order from the smallest to the largest.

1.   8,324   5,843
      58,488
       5,843
      54,388

2.   679,299
       6,279
      69,599
     675,922

Read each clue and write the numerals in the crossword puzzle.

ACROSS

1. One million, six hundred thousand, four hundred, and fifty
2. Thirty-three thousand, nine hundred, and seventy-two
3. Nine thousand, nine hundred, and sixty-eight

DOWN

1. Ten thousand, eight hundred, and ninety-nine
4. Three hundred and two thousand, three hundred, and forty-six
5. Four hundred and eighty-nine
6. Seven hundred and eighty-eight
7. One thousand and fifty-two

Constitution Connection

All the words or phrases on the left have to do with the US Constitution. Draw a line to match each one with the correct description on the right.

1. Preamble

2. Articles

3. Amendments

4. Constitutional Convention

5. Articles of Confederation

6. Ratify

7. Separation of Powers

8. Framers

a) The meeting at which delegates from all the colonies discussed how the United States should be governed

b) Changes or additions to the Constitution. The first ten are called the Bill of Rights.

c) To vote on and approve a change to the Constitution

d) The opening section of the US Constitution. It describes the purpose of the Constitution and the role of the government.

e) There are seven of these in the US Constitution. They explain how the government is structured.

f) The people who wrote and planned the Constitution, such as Benjamin Franklin, James Madison, George Washington, and others

g) Power is divided up among three branches of government.

h) The United States was governed by this document before the Constitution was written.

Early or Late?

Look at the time on each clock. Is the person early or late? Circle your answer.

1. Maya's dance class starts in 2 hours, 10 minutes. She got to class at 4:45.

EARLY   (LATE)

2. The Joneses will eat dinner in 1 hour, 30 minutes. Steven sat down to eat at 6:05.

EARLY   LATE

3. Open House is in 3 hours, 40 minutes. Melissa's parents got to the room at 7:20.

EARLY   LATE

4. Marcus walks the dog in 2 hours, 40 minutes. He will leave at 9:00.

EARLY   LATE

5. The softball game is in 4 hours, 20 minutes. Tham will take the field at 5:50.

EARLY   LATE

6. The talent show starts at 7:30. Leah will arrive in 2 hours, 15 minutes.

EARLY   LATE

7. School ends in 3 hours, 30 minutes. Dan's swim meet begins $\frac{1}{2}$ hour after school. Dan will get to the meet at 3:05.

EARLY   LATE

8. Morgan's shift begins in 4 hours, 20 minutes. She will get to work at 1:00 on the dot.

EARLY   LATE

9. The birthday party begins in 3 hours, 35 minutes. Jenny will get to the party at 12:45.

EARLY   LATE

10. Jack will get to baseball camp in $4\frac{1}{2}$ hours. Camp lasts for $6\frac{1}{2}$ hours. Camp ends at 6:45 PM.

EARLY   LATE

Giants of the Sea

Read the article. Then answer the questions below.

There are about 75 different kinds of whales. They are the largest animals in the ocean. In fact, the blue whale is the largest animal in the world. Blues whales aren't really blue. They are more of a gray-blue with whitish speckles. A blue whale grows to about 80 feet long and weighs about 120 tons. Its heart is the size of a small car and weighs about 1,000 pounds. The blue whale is also the loudest animal on earth. Blue whales talk to each other through whistles. These whistles can reach levels up to 188 decibels and can be heard for hundreds of miles. The sound of a jet engine is only 140 decibels!

Blue whales are baleen whales. This means that they filter tiny plankton and fish from the water. They are called "gulpers" because they gulp mouthfuls of plankton or fish as they swim. Fifty to seventy throat pleats allow the throat to expand and form a large pouch. The water is then forced through the baleen plates hanging from the upper jaw. The baleen acts like a sieve catching the food. A blue whale will eat 2,000 to 9,000 pounds of plankton each day during the summer feeding season.

1. How many different kinds of whales are there? _____ about 75 _____

2. How big does a blue whale grow to be? _____

3. How do blue whales talk to each other? _____

4. Is a blue whale louder than a lion? _____
How do you know? _____

_____

_____

5. What is a baleen whale? _____

_____

_____

6. Explain how a blue whale feeds. _____

_____

_____

A Summery Summary

Read about Sarah's summer vacation. Then read the summaries and circle the best one.

Sarah had the best summer vacation ever! She went to Hawaii with her family. Sarah went to the beach every day. She learned how to snorkel and saw lots of pretty fish in all different colors. One day she even saw a sea turtle while she was snorkeling. Sarah's favorite part of the trip happened on the last night. She and her family went to a special dinner and show called a luau. They watched dancers in hula skirts while they ate dinner. What a treat!

Summary A

Sarah's favorite part of this trip to Hawaii was the luau. The luau included a delicious dinner and a great show. She really liked watching all the hula dancers. What a great way to end this summer vacation!

Summary B

Sarah went to the beach every day when she was in Hawaii. She learned how to snorkel so that she could see all the colorful fish. She even saw a sea turtle one day while she was snorkeling.

Summary C

Sarah went to Hawaii with her family for her summer vacation. She saw colorful fish and a sea turtle while she was snorkeling. Sarah's favorite part of the trip was the luau that she went to on her last night.

On a separate piece of paper write a summary of what you've done so far on your summer vacation. Remember, a summary doesn't include all the details. It just gives the main ideas.

Party Punch

Follow the directions below.

This Party Punch has two recipe cards. Look at the first ingredient. $2\frac{1}{3}$ and $\frac{7}{3}$ are the same, but one is a proper fraction and one is an improper fraction. Convert the fraction for each ingredient to complete the cards.

Proper Punch

$2\frac{1}{3}$ tablespoons strawberry punch powder mix

1. _____ cups sugar

$8\frac{1}{2}$ cups cold water

2. _____ cups orange sherbet

$2\frac{1}{3}$ cups ginger ale

3. _____ cups pineapple juice

$4\frac{3}{4}$ cups orange juice

Improper Punch

$\frac{7}{3}$ tablespoons strawberry punch powder mix

$\frac{5}{4}$ cups sugar

4. _____ cups cold water

$\frac{14}{3}$ cups orange sherbet

5. _____ cups ginger ale

$\frac{19}{4}$ cups pineapple juice

6. _____ cups orange juice

Starry Skies

Multiply. Then cross out the stars with the answers.

2	9	12	4	6	10
× 2	× 9	× 12	× 4	× 6	× 10

11	5	1	3	8	7
× 11	× 5	× 1	× 3	× 8	× 7

72   144   4   9   12   16   25   36

81   49   1   100   121   64   30   18

How many stars are left in the sky? _____

Make It Better

Read each simple sentence. Can you make the situation better?

Turn each simple sentence into a compound sentence by adding a conjunction and another sentence part. Use the conjunctions in the box to help you. Remember to use a comma before a conjunction in a compound sentence.

> **Example:** My bike is broken.
> My bike is broken, but my dad is driving me to school.

> **Conjunctions**
> although   yet   and   but   or

1. I lost my backpack at the museum.

_____

2. My lunchbox is full of bugs.

_____

3. I dropped my homework in the mud.

_____

4. I ripped a hole in my jeans.

_____

5. My pet bird flew out of its cage.

_____

6. The class field trip is canceled.

_____

7. I spilled juice on my shirt.

_____

8. The puppy chewed up my shoes.

_____

9. Our team lost the game.

_____

10. I can't go out and play in the rain.

_____

Tic-Tac-Toe

Follow the directions below.

Circle the row in which all the fractions and decimals are equal.
Don't forget to check the diagonal rows!

1.

.4	$\frac{4}{1}$	$\frac{4}{10}$
.40	$\frac{4}{100}$	.04
$\frac{4}{10}$	.4	$\frac{4}{100}$

(The first column is circled)

2.

.06	$\frac{6}{1}$	$\frac{60}{100}$
$\frac{60}{10}$	6.0	$\frac{6}{10}$
$\frac{60}{100}$	$\frac{6}{10}$	.6

3.

.2	$\frac{1}{2}$	$\frac{2}{10}$
.02	$\frac{2}{100}$	$\frac{20}{1000}$
$\frac{2}{1}$	$\frac{22}{100}$	2.2

4.

.05	$\frac{1}{2}$	5.0
$\frac{5}{10}$	$\frac{5}{100}$	$\frac{20}{1000}$
.5	$\frac{1}{5}$	$\frac{1}{20}$

Write each decimal as a fraction.

5.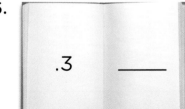

.3 _____

6.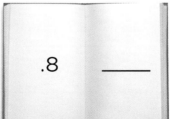

.8 _____

7.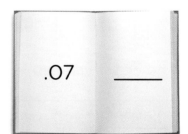

.07 _____

Write each fraction as a decimal.

8.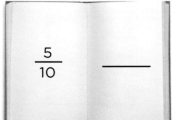

$\frac{5}{10}$ _____

9.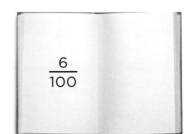

$\frac{6}{100}$ _____

10.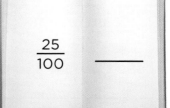

$\frac{25}{100}$ _____

Adding and Subtracting Decimals

Add or subtract. Use placeholders.

1.   26.7
     + 18.1
     ‾‾‾‾‾
     44.8

2.   93.6
     − 2.9
     ‾‾‾‾‾

3.   7.30
     + 19.6
     ‾‾‾‾‾

4. 62.79
     + 3.15
     ‾‾‾‾‾

5. 87.50
     − 3.47
     ‾‾‾‾‾

6. 42.55
     − 1.7
     ‾‾‾‾‾

7. 86. 9
     + 10.25
     ‾‾‾‾‾

8. 51.07
     − 3.03
     ‾‾‾‾‾

9.   4.67
     + 18.36
     ‾‾‾‾‾

10. 27.5
     + 4.33
     ‾‾‾‾‾

11. 37.88
     − 26.04
     ‾‾‾‾‾

12. 99.73
     − 78.80
     ‾‾‾‾‾

What Is the Genre?

There are many different kinds of stories. These different types of stories are called **genres**. Look at the genres in the box. Then read each passage below. Write the genre on the line.

Genres

fiction	nonfiction	fairy tale	myth	tall tale
fable	biography	poetry	mystery	science fiction

USA 33

JACKIE ROBINSON

1. Jorge is reading a book about the life of baseball player Jackie Robinson. He is learning about the struggles Robinson faced as the first African American to play in the major leagues. What genre is it?_____biography_____

2. Alex is reading a story that has been passed down from long ago. This story tells how the ancient Greeks thought their gods made the seasons change. Alex's favorite god is Apollo, god of the sun. What genre is it? _____

3. Kate is reading a story about a princess who loses her magic sword. A fairy helps the princess realize she can fight the evil dragon with her own powers, without the sword. What genre is it? _____

4. Suri is reading a story about a famous TV pet that goes missing. When the owners find out that it's been kidnapped, they follow clues that lead them into many adventures. What genre is it?_____

5. Emilio is reading a story about a girl who transports herself into the future through her computer. She discovers people living on Mars and traveling with lasers. What genre is it? _____

6. Lauren is reading a story about a proud, selfish pig that won't share its slop with the other pigs. In the end, the pig learns a hard lesson about sharing that everyone can learn from. What genre is it?_____

Now, write a description of a story that fits one of the genres in the box.

_____
_____
_____

What genre is it?_____

Fact or Opinion?

A **fact** is true and can be proven. An **opinion** is how you feel about something.

Example:
Fact: The beach is 1.2 miles from my house.
Opinion: The beach is too hot today.

Write **F** for **fact** and **O** for **opinion** for each statement below.

1. In the Middle Ages, many people lived in castles for protection. ____F____

2. Stone castles replaced wooden ones because they wouldn't burn. _____

3. A stone castle would feel cold during the winter. _____

4. Most people preferred to live in castles rather than in small villages. _____

5. Minstrels and jugglers performed for the king and queen. _____

6. Banquets and plays were the favorite amusements of the day. _____

7. A castle's outer walls were usually about 12 feet thick. _____

8. Enemy armies camped outside castle walls until people began to starve. _____

9. It was probably frightening to be trapped inside a castle. _____

10. Prisoners of war were kept inside castle basements, called dungeons. _____

Write a fact and an opinion about what it was like to live in the Middle Ages.

Fact: _____

Opinion: _____

Multiplication Marathon

Multiply to solve each problem. See how fast you can finish all the problems!

1.   452
    × 5
    ‾‾‾‾
    2260

2.   235
    × 6
    ‾‾‾‾

3.   338
    × 4
    ‾‾‾‾

4.   12
    × 12
    ‾‾‾‾

5.   58
    × 13
    ‾‾‾‾

6.   45
    × 22
    ‾‾‾‾

7.   231
    × 14
    ‾‾‾‾

8.   664
    × 11
    ‾‾‾‾

9.   173
    × 25
    ‾‾‾‾

10. 525
    × 10
    ‾‾‾‾

11. 226
    × 34
    ‾‾‾‾

12. 709
    × 82
    ‾‾‾‾

Dare to Divide

Follow the directions below.

Solve each word problem. Write the answer on the line.

1. Mr. Glick paid $121 for tickets to the zoo. There are 11 people in the class. How much was each ticket?

_$11_

2. Kate gives $144 to an animal charity each year. She gives the same amount each month. How much does she give each month? _____

3. Megan has collected 150 marbles. She divided them evenly into 10 bags. How many marbles are in each bag?

_____

4. Seashore Community has 240 homes. There are 12 homes in each neighborhood. How many neighborhoods are in Seashore Community? _____

5. Brian counted 70 new puppies at the animal shelter. Each dog had 5 puppies. How many dogs are at the shelter?

_____

6. Sam baked 108 cupcakes for the bake sale. She sold them all in 3 hours. If she sold the same number of cupcakes each hour, how many did she sell per hour?

_____

Write out each answer from above in word form.

1. ___ ( ) ___ ( ) ___ ___

2. ___ ( ) ___ ___ ___ ( )

3. ( ) ___ ___ ( ) ___ ___ ___

4. ___ ( ) ___ ___ ___ ( )

5. ___ ___ ( ) ___ ___ ___ ___ ___

6. ___ ___ ___ ___ ___ ___ - ( ) ___ ___

To solve the riddle, find the circled letters in the secret code. Write the corresponding letters, in order, on the lines below.

E = F	F = D	I = S	N = R
R = M	S = R	V = A	Y = L
X = N	H = E	L = H	U = A
W = L	T = O		

Riddle: What coin doubles in value when half is deducted?

Answer: A ___ ___ ___ ___   ___ ___ ___ ___ ___ ___

33

Guide Words

Do you know how to find words in a dictionary or thesaurus?
They are listed in alphabetical order.

Two words appear at the top of each page. They are called **guide words.**
- The first guide word is the first word on the page.
- The second guide word is the last word on the page.

Look at the guide words on each page. Then circle the words that would appear on that page. There could be one, two, or three.

1.

might mirth	shame shear
melon	sheet
milk	shark
mitten	share

2.

brain break	always aunt
brawl	among
breathe	after
brake	author

3.

smoke story	child choice
speaker	choose
storm	chilly
snail	china

4.

present price	wander weather
pretty	wanted
precious	walkway
private	wasteful

5.

endless engine	found function
elephant	foundation
engage	friendly
enemy	fulcrum

6.

refer return	laugh litter
regal	logic
rewind	lively
really	lawful

7.

king known	jeer jester
kingdom	jeep
knoll	jagged
kick	jelly

8.

spoil spring	droop dump
spread	dugout
sprig	dragon
spool	drown

9.

park parse	closet clover
parent	cloud
parkway	clumsy
parrot	clothing

Division Days

Solve each division problem and find the answer at the bottom.
Some of the answers have remainders. Write the letter on the line and you'll solve the riddle!

S	L	E	Z	W	A	O
9)5868	7)321	5)982	2)308	9)376	8)387	6)480

N	I	D	T	S	A	A
4)185	7)406	2)522	3)752	8)168	4)565	5)75

Why was the calendar so confused?

It ___ ___ ___   ___ ___ ___ ___   ___ ___ ___
41 R7 15 652   45 R6 80 21 250 R2   58 46 R1 141 R1

___ ___ ___ ___ .
261 48 R3 154 196 R2

Postcard from the Past

Follow the directions below.

Think about the history of the state where you live. Choose a specific time in the past and imagine what it was like to live during that time. Write a postcard to someone describing what life was like in your state. You can use an encyclopedia or another reference book for help.

Use these questions to help you think about the history of your state.
Who lived in your state before Columbus arrived?
Why did people begin moving to your state, or how did they get there?
How did your state gain statehood?
Were there any wars or conflicts that took place in your state?
What kinds of jobs did people have?
Where did most people live?
What are some special features of your state?

Shapes around Us

Shapes can be moved in different ways. The shape doesn't change, but it looks different. There are shapes all around us in everything we see.

1. Look at this shape. If you turn it upside down, what will it look like? Draw the shape.

2. Look at this shape. If you turn it once to the left, what will it look like? Draw the shape.

3. What is this shape? _____ Draw an object of the same shape.

4. What is this shape? _____ Draw an object of the same shape.

5. What is this shape? _____ Draw an object of the same shape.

6. What is this shape? _____ Draw an object of the same shape.

Bite into That

Read through the paragraph and find the sentences that give **facts** and sentences that give the author's **opinions**. Write the sentences below.

A shark's teeth are its most amazing feature! Humans have only one row of teeth on the top and the bottom. A shark's mouth is more interesting because it has many rows of teeth. Whenever a shark loses a tooth, a new one moves forward to replace it. A shark goes through thousands of teeth in its lifetime. It would be great if human teeth could replace themselves like that! Sharks use their sharp teeth to catch food, but sometimes they accidentally bite into something that's not food, such as metal! In fact, scientists have found tin cans inside sharks' stomachs. So, people need to be careful not to litter or throw cans into the ocean. One shark is actually named after its giant teeth. The "Megalodon," which means "big tooth," is an ancient shark that had six-inch teeth. Since the Megalodon lived millions of years ago, we don't know what it looked like. With teeth that big, it must have been an awesome sight. It would definitely scare me away!

Facts

_____

_____

_____

_____

_____

Opinions

_____

_____

_____

_____

_____

_____

Rocky Riddles

Read each riddle and find the answer in the box.
Write the answer to the riddle on the line.

calcite   metamorphic   feldspar
igneous   sedimentary   quartz

1.
I am a mineral with six-sided crystals.
I am so hard, I can scratch steel. I am
used in jewelry and glass.

_____quartz_____

2.
I am so soft, I can be scratched with a
penny. I am white, yellow, or sometimes
transparent. I am used in toothpaste,
chewing gum, glue, and soap.

_____

3.
I am the most common of all minerals.
I have flat sides. I come in many colors,
like pink, white, and green.

_____

4.
I come from volcanoes! When lava
cools, it hardens into rock. That's how
I'm made.

_____

5.
I have many layers called strata. Each
layer is made from tiny rocks that
formed together. That's how I'm made.

_____

6.
I am a rock that has undergone a
change. Heat and pressure turn me into
something new. That's how I'm made.

_____

The Summer of Clubs

Read the story. Then follow the directions.

Scott and Steve played together every summer. Then one summer, Steve's cousin Henry came to visit. Scott was worried that Steve would spend all of his time with Henry, so Scott came up with a plan to keep Steve to himself.

Scott decided to start the Tree House Club. He knew that Henry was afraid of heights, so he planned to have the club meet in a tree house. Scott asked Steve to join the club.

"That sounds great," said Steve. "But my cousin Henry won't be able to climb into the tree house. Can he still be in the club?"

"Sorry," Scott said, "but those are the club rules. If he doesn't want to go in the tree house, then he can't be in the club. Besides, you don't have to do everything with Henry."

Steve agreed to join the club. He had a lot of fun playing with Scott in the tree house, but Henry felt left out. Steve started to feel guilty about leaving his cousin all alone.

Steve came up with a plan, too. He and Henry started the Island Club. They planned to swim across the lake and have meetings on an island. They asked Scott to join.

"But I don't know how to swim," Scott said. "Can I still be in the club?"

"Sorry, but no," said Steve. "Those are the club rules."

Steve and Henry had a lot of fun swimming to the island. Scott looked on sadly. Now he understood what it was like to be left out.

"I have an idea," he told Steve and Henry. "Let's start a new club together. We'll call it the Fun Club! The only rule is that we all have fun together and don't leave anybody out."

Steve and Henry agreed. In fact, they found that they could have even more fun with three people!

Write some words that describe each character.

Scott

_____

_____

_____

Steve

_____

_____

_____

Henry

_____

_____

_____

Clubs Continued

Refer to the story on page 40 to fill in the information.

The Tree House Club

1. Club Members: _____

2. Who started this club and why? _____

_____

3. Club Rule: _____

What happened because of this rule?

_____

_____

_____

The Island Club

4. Club Members: _____

5. Who started this club and why? _____

_____

_____

6. Club Rule: _____

What happened because of this rule?

_____

_____

_____

The Fun Club

7. Club Members: _____

8. Who started this club and why? _____

_____

9. Club Rule: _____

What happened because of this rule?

_____

_____

_____

Laura's Lunch

Plug each set of numbers into the equation below. If the number pair makes a true equation, color the box. If not, don't color the box. Try all the number pairs to figure out which meal Laura had for lunch!

$$3 + a = b$$

a = 4 b = 7 3 + 4 = 7	a = 3 b = 6	a = 3 b = 9	a = 5 b = 15
a = 2 b = 6	a = 12 b = 15	a = 10 b = 13	a = 11 b = 15
a = 2 b = 1	a = 8 b = 12	a = 6 b = 9	a = 1 b = 4

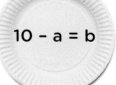

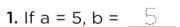

10 – a = b

a + 7 = b

1. If a = 5, b = ___5___

2. If a = 9, b = _____

3. If b = 4, a = _____

4. If b = 7, a = _____

5. If a = 3, b = _____

6. If a = 7, b = _____

7. If b = 9, a = _____

8. If b = 20, a = _____

Circle Graph

Marco is doing a class survey. He wants to find out his classmates' favorite sweet treats. He put his results in a circle graph.

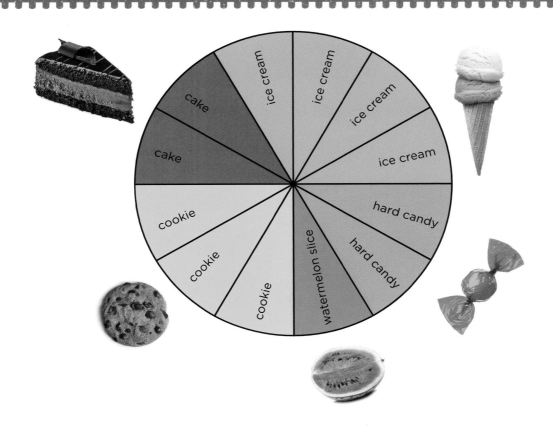

Answer the questions about the circle graph.
Hint: Each section of the circle stands for 4 students.

1. What fraction of the students likes ice cream? $\frac{1}{3}$ _____

2. How many students like cookies? _____

3. How many more students like ice cream than fruit? _____

4. What fraction of students like cake? _____

5. What fraction of students like cookies? _____

6. How many students like cookies, cake, and fruit? _____

7. Which two sweets do the same amount of students like? _____

8. How many students were surveyed altogether? _____

Hurray for Holidays!

Proper nouns are words that include the names of countries and people, days of the week, months of the year, and holidays. All proper nouns are capitalized. Use the letter code to fill in each word. Use capital letters correctly.

A	B	C	D	E	F	G	H	I	J	K	L	M	N	O	P	Q	R	S	T	U	V	W	X	Y	Z
1	2	3	4	5	6	7	8	9	10	11	12	13	14	15	16	17	18	19	20	21	22	23	24	25	26

People around the world celebrate different holidays. For example, at the beginning of every lunar year, the C h i n e s e (3 8 9 14 5 19 5) celebrate their new year. Each new year is represented by a different animal. The year 2015 is the year of the __ __ __ __ (7 15 1 20).

In the __ __ __ __ __ __ (23 9 14 20 5 18), many families around the world celebrate __ __ __ __ __ __ __ __ __ (3 8 18 9 19 20 13 1 19). They buy pine trees and stuff stockings with treats and toys. Winter is also the time when __ __ __ __ __ __ (10 5 23 9 19 8) people celebrate __ __ __ __ __ __ __ __ (8 1 14 21 11 11 1 8). This holiday is also known as "the festival of __ __ __ __ __ __ (12 9 7 8 20 19)." Another important holiday takes place in __ __ __ __ __ __ (13 5 24 9 3 15). The people of this country celebrate their 1862 victory over the French army in the Battle of __ __ __ __ __ __ (16 21 5 2 12 1). People have fun by eating traditional Mexican foods and dancing. One of the favorite __ __ __ __ __ __ __ __ (1 13 5 18 9 3 1 14) holidays has always been __ __ __ __ __ __ __ __ __ __ __ __ (20 8 1 14 11 19 7 9 22 9 14 7). On this day, families gather together to celebrate their good fortune and eat a traditional __ __ __ __ (13 5 1 12), including a big __ __ __ __ __ __ (20 21 18 11 5 25) and mashed potatoes. Holidays are special because they allow people from different __ __ __ __ __ __ __ __ __ (3 15 21 14 20 18 9 5 19) to honor their history and culture. What holidays does your family celebrate?

Shape Crossword

Read the clues to guess each shape.
Write the names of the shapes in the puzzle.

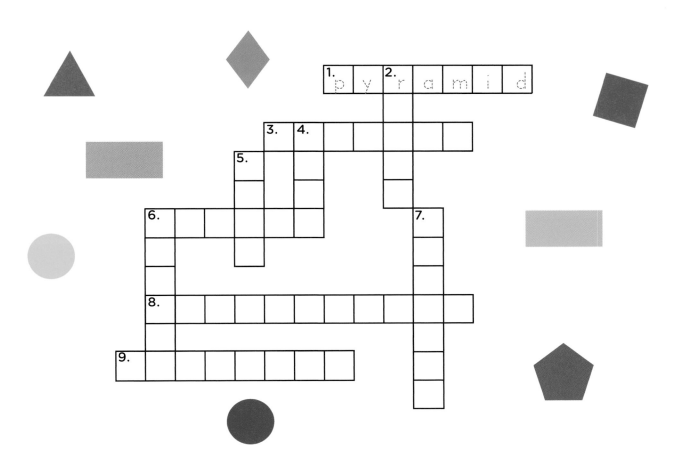

ACROSS

1. I look like a triangle from the front, but I have 5 surfaces. What shape am I?

3. I have 8 equal sides and 8 equal angles. What shape am I?

6. I have 4 equal sides and 4 equal angles. What shape am I?

8. I am a triangle with 3 equal sides. What kind of triangle am I?

9. I am a polygon with 5 equal sides and 5 equal angles. What shape am I?

DOWN

2. I am a triangle with one 90° angle. What kind of triangle am I?

4. I look square from the front, but I have 6 surfaces. What shape am I?

5. I am round, but I'm not a circle. You see me in an egg. What shape am I?

6. I am round. You see me in a beach ball or globe. What shape am I?

7. I am a polygon with 6 equal sides and 6 equal angles. What shape am I?

Meeting the Challenge

A personal narrative is a real-life story about you. It tells about an experience you've had through descriptive details and events. You are the main character!

Think about a time when you were scared or anxious about something. Maybe you were giving a presentation in class or moving to a new neighborhood or school. Think about how you felt and how you met the challenge. Write a personal narrative telling about this event. Provide vivid details to "paint a picture" for the reader. Describe what you felt, saw, and heard.

Title: _____

_____

_____

_____

_____

_____

_____

_____

_____

_____

_____

_____

_____

_____

_____

_____

Follow the Signs

Solve each equation. Remember to do the problem inside the parentheses first.

1. $3(4 + 5) =$ _27_

2. $5(7 + 2) =$ _____

3. $8(6 - 4)$ _____

4. $2(10 + 2) =$ _____

5. $8(5 - 4) =$ _____

6. $1(6 + 5) =$ _____

7. $4(8 - 3) =$ _____

8. $7(3 + 7) =$ _____

Divide and Conquer

Find the two numbers in each chart that can be used to complete the division problem. Cross out the numbers you don't use. Then write the problem.

1.

9	12	72
36	14	10

_____ ÷ 8 = _____

2.

18	7	24
9	4	28

_____ ÷ _____ = 2

3.

81	84	77
10	8	12

_____ ÷ 7 = _____

4.

10	5	8
7	11	6

56 ÷ _____ = _____

5.

25	12	45
15	5	8

_____ ÷ _____ = 9

6.

70	6	100
60	95	17

_____ ÷ 10 = _____

7.

7	16	21
4	15	9

_____ ÷ 3 = _____

8.

12	6	14
2	8	11

88 ÷ _____ = _____

9.

3	30	6
24	5	32

_____ ÷ _____ = 6

10.

12	144	132
99	10	1

_____ ÷ 11 = _____

11.

7	9	4
6	5	15

54 ÷ _____ = _____

12.

56	96	6
64	9	8

_____ ÷ 8 = _____

Perfect Punctuation

Read this story. Add the missing punctuation marks.

- Add **quotation marks** around spoken words.
- Add **commas** between words in a series.
- Add a **period** at the end of statements.
- Add a **question mark** at the end of questions.
- Add an **exclamation mark** at the end of sentences that show strong feeling.

Time to get up   Dad called   Maggie and Brett dragged themselves out of the tent   Dad grinned at their sleepy faces

Are you ready for our hike   he asked

Brett groaned   Why do we have to go so early   he whined

Most of the wildlife is out in the morning   Dad explained   I promise you won't be sorry

I'm already sorry   Maggie complained, rubbing the sleep out of her eyes

After eating a good breakfast, they hit the trail with Dad in the lead   A fine gray mist hung over the mountain   Maggie breathed in the smell of wet leaves   pine trees   and wildflowers   Dad was right   Morning on the mountain was beautiful   Brett wasn't so sure   He dragged his feet and kicked rocks along the trail

Would you like to stop up there in that meadow to have a snack   Dad asked

I don't care   Brett grumbled

What a grump   Maggie teased

In the meadow, the hikers sat on a big rock while they snacked on berries   nuts and raisins

Be very quiet   Dad whispered   We might see something really special Brett was doubtful   Suddenly Maggie grabbed his arm and pointed to the edge of the forest   A mother deer and her fawn stood silently, watching them   Then the deer slowly walked into the meadow to feed on fresh green grass   Wow Brett could hardly believe his eyes

After the deer left the meadow, Dad turned to Maggie and Brett   What did you think   Dad asked with a smile

That was amazing   Brett exclaimed   You were right   This was worth getting up for

It's Shocking!

Read about the differences between static electricity and current electricity. Then think of examples of each type of electricity and list them below.

Static Electricity

A buildup of electrons

Stays in one place and jumps to an object

Does not need a circuit

Examples: Lightning; when you drag your feet across carpet and touch something

Current Electricity

Steady flow of electrons

Needs a conductor (like a wire)

Needs a circuit

Examples: batteries, outlet plugs

Static Electricity

_____

_____

_____

Current Electricity

_____

_____

_____

Batter Up!

Multiply or divide. Then tell if the first product is **less than**, **greater than**, or **equal to** the second product by writing **<**, **>**, or **=** in the baseballs.

1. 9 × 9  10 × 8

2. 5 × 5 4 × 7

3. 8 × 7 6 × 11

4. 3 × 4 12 × 1

5. 12 × 9 10 × 10

6. 4 × 8 7 × 6

7. 6 × 9 11 × 5

8. 3 × 8 5 × 4

9. 4 × 4 8 × 2

10. 10 × 2 6 × 3

11. 7 × 7 8 × 5

12. 3 × 12 6 × 6

13. 6 × 10 12 × 5

14. 5 × 9 12 × 4

15. 8 × 8 9 × 7

16. 5 × 3 7 × 2

Vivid Verbs

Verbs are action words. They tell the action in a sentence.
Verb tense can be **present**, **past**, or **past participle**. Read the examples.

Examples:

Present Tense	Past Tense	Past Participle
bring	brought	brought
speak	spoke	spoken
fall	fell	fallen
throw	threw	thrown

Read each sentence. Then rewrite it using the tense
in ( ). The first one is done for you.

1. Maya fell off her bike and scraped her knee. (past participle)
   Maya had fallen off her bike and scraped her knee.

2. Emma and Sam eat eggs and toast for breakfast. (past tense)
   _____

3. Alonzo rode the bus to school each day. (present tense)
   _____

4. I am using the computer to do my research. (past participle)
   _____

5. The lizard had been running along the fence. (present tense)
   _____

6. Spring flowers bloom outside my bedroom window. (past tense)
   _____

7. The earthquake shook the jars off the shelf onto the floor. (past participle)
   _____

8. Chloe had swum the race with the fastest time. (present tense)
   _____

9. Dad drives us to the mall every Saturday. (past tense)
   _____

10. I chose a great big chocolate sundae for dessert. (past participle)
    _____

Amazing American Women

Compare and contrast by filling in the Venn diagram below. In the middle of the diagram, write some things that Abigail Adams and Mercy Otis Warren have in common. In the other parts, write about things that are unique to each woman.

Abigail Adams

Abigail Adams was an important leader in America's fight for independence. Abigail wanted America to break away from England and become its own country. Her husband, John Adams, was often away helping with the American Revolution. Abigail raised the children and ran the farm by herself. She wrote many letters to her husband, sharing her opinions about independence. She also felt strongly about improving the treatment of women during this time. When John was helping to write the nation's new constitution, Abigail wrote to him to remind him about the importance of women's rights. Abigail and John both enjoyed reading and writing about politics. John was vice president to George Washington and then was elected as the second president of the United States. Abigail was a partner to and supporter of her husband.

Mercy Otis Warren

Mercy Otis Warren helped support the Revolutionary War through her writing. Mercy believed strongly that America should gain independence from England. She became a patriot writer; and she wrote plays, poems, articles, and books that supported independence. Mercy also felt passionately about women's rights. She thought it was wrong that women were not seen as equal to men during this time. Mercy married James Warren, and together they enjoyed reading, writing, and discussing politics. James was elected to the Massachusetts House of Representatives during the Revolution. Mercy supported her husband and continued to write about independence.

Abigail Adams   Mercy Otis Warren

_____   _____   _____
_____   _____   _____
_____   _____   _____
_____   _____   _____
_____   _____   _____

Figure It Out

Follow the directions below.

Congruent shapes are the same size and shape. Circle the sets of figures that are congruent.

a.

b.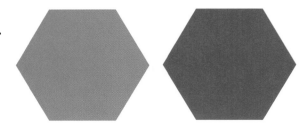

c.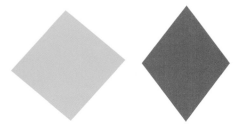

d.

Symmetry means that a shape is made of two sides that are exactly the same. Circle the figures that are symmetrical.

a.

b.

c.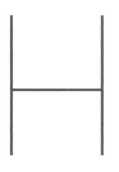

d.

School Days

Use multiplication or division to solve each word problem. Read each problem carefully to make sure you know what it's asking you to do. Hint: Solving some problems will depend on answers or information from previous problems.

1. Our school has 600 students and 20 classrooms. If there is an equal number of students in each classroom, how many students are in each classroom? 30

2. Half of the students take buses to school, and 35 students fit on each bus. What is the least number of buses needed to take students to school each day? _____

3. One-third of the students sold cookies in the bake sale. If each student sold $25 worth of cookies, how much money did they make? _____

4. Each class takes two field trips in the fall and two field trips in the spring. How many field trips do all the classes take per year? _____

5. Each teacher needs 12 packs of pencils and 4 packs of notebooks for each class. How many packs of each does the school need to order for all the teachers?

_____

6. One-sixth of the students are in the school talent show. If each pair of students is putting on one skit, how many skits will be performed? _____

7. Each student must attend 5 classes per day. How many classes does one class of students attend in one normal school week? _____

8. Mr. Beck coaches 6 soccer teams and 3 tennis teams. Each soccer team has 15 players. Each tennis team has 12 players. How many players does Mr. Beck coach altogether? _____

The Main Idea

Read each paragraph. Circle the topic sentence and
underline two supporting details.

- The **main idea** tells what a paragraph is mostly about.
- You can usually find the main idea in the **topic sentence**. This sentence tells the most important idea in a paragraph. It usually comes at the beginning or the end of a paragraph.
- **Details** are pieces of information that expand on the main idea. Details help you see a clear picture of the main idea.

1. Poison dart frogs are beautiful but dangerous. They don't bite or sting. Instead, they have poison glands all over their bodies. When a poison dart frog is scared, poison oozes out of its skin. This poison is one of the most toxic in the world.

2. The president of the United States has a very hard job, but at least there are people who help with some duties. These people are called the Cabinet. The president gets to choose members of the Cabinet. Each member looks over a part of the government. Some of these include departments of Homeland Security, Education, and Justice.

3. The upper edge of the Grand Canyon is forested with trees, bushes, and cacti. Every layer of the canyon contains some kind of life. You can see mule deer, coyotes, bighorn sheep, bats, and all kinds of snakes. More than 300 species of birds live there. The Grand Canyon is filled with all forms of life, from the top to the bottom.

4. Saturn is a unique planet because of its system of bright rings. The rings are so bright, they are fairly easy to see through a telescope. Saturn's rings are made of millions of small particles that orbit the planet together. They are distinct and appear continuous in nature.

Angles and Lines

Follow the directions below.

Use the **<**, **>**, or **=** symbol to show whether each angle is **less than**, **greater than**, or **equal to** 90 degrees.

Label each set of lines as **perpendicular** or **parallel**.

1.

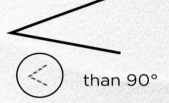

(**<**) than 90°

2.

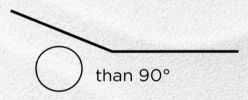

( ) than 90°

3.

( ) than 90°

4.

( ) than 90°

5.

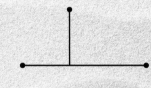

parallel

6.

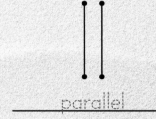

7.

8.

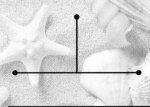

Branching Out

See the graph. Then follow the directions below.

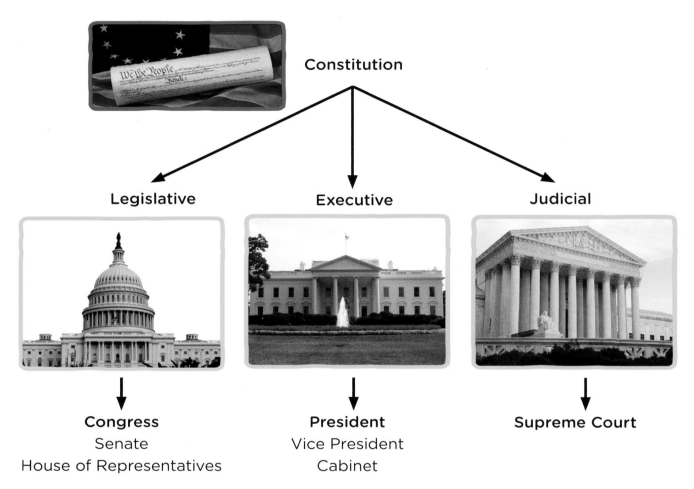

Constitution

Legislative

Executive

Judicial

Congress
Senate
House of Representatives

President
Vice President
Cabinet

Supreme Court

Connect each definition with the correct word. Use the diagram above for help.

1. A group of people who advise and help the president.
2. A body of lawmakers made up of the Senate and the House of Representatives
3. The branch of government that makes up the court system
4. The head of the executive branch
5. The document that explains how the government is structured
6. The branch of government that makes laws through Congress
7. The president is the head of this branch
8. The highest court in the nation

a) Constitution
b) Legislative
c) Executive
d) Judicial
e) Supreme Court
f) President
g) Congress
h) Cabinet

Graph It!

How many astronauts have walked on the moon? Follow the directions below.
The answer will appear in the graph! Hint: The first number in each coordinate is on the x-axis.

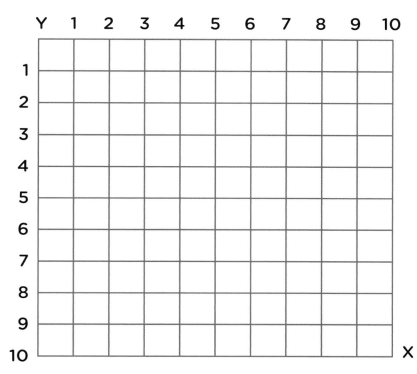

Draw a colored dot on each coordinate:

1. Green (8,3)　　**2.** Green (6,6)　　**3.** Blue (3,4)　　**4.** Green (5,4)

5. Green (5,7)　　**6.** Green (6,3)　　**7.** Blue (3,6)　　**8.** Green (7,5)

9. Green (8,7)　　**10.** Green (6,7)　　**11.** Blue (2,4)　　**12.** Blue (3,5)

13. Green (8,4)　　**14.** Green (7,7)　　**15.** Blue (3,3)　　**16.** Blue (3,7)

Draw a green line to connect the green dots. Draw a blue
line to connect the blue dots.

Answer: _____ astronauts have walked on the moon!

Cause and Effect

A **cause** is why something happens. An **effect** is what happens as a result of the cause. Read the passage. Then answer the questions.

It was 1955 when Rosa Parks climbed onto a bus for a ride home. She was tired from a long day at work. When she took a seat near the front of the bus, she was asked to move. When she didn't, she was arrested. What had she done wrong? Rosa Parks was African American. In 1955, African Americans did not have the same rights as white people. Some of the rules stated that African Americans were not allowed to go to the same schools as whites or drink out of the same water fountains. They also had to sit in the backs of buses. On this day, however, Rosa Parks refused to move. Sick of the injustice, she stayed in her seat and was arrested for it. This one act of courage would change the nation forever. Other African Americans started a bus boycott in protest. They stopped taking the buses and walked or used carpools instead. This hurt the bus business and brought the civil rights movement into full force. This one act of courage helped change the laws of the city as well as of the nation.

1. What do you think caused Rosa Parks to stay in her seat?

_____

_____

2. What was the effect of Rosa Parks being arrested?

_____

_____

3. How did the Montgomery bus boycott affect the bus business?

_____

_____

4. Describe the long-term effect of Rosa Parks's brave act. How do you think it affected the city of Montgomery? How do you think it affected the nation?

_____

_____

_____

_____

5. Do you know someone else who did something brave or stood up for a good cause? On another piece of paper, write about this person. Tell what he or she did and why you respect him or her.

Volcano Vocabulary

Find the word that completes each sentence.

magma

lava

crust

dormant

active

mantle

erupt

pressure

What makes a volcano 1) _erupt_ ? It all starts deep within the Earth. The top

layer of Earth is called the 2) _____ . Below the crust is a layer of hot rock called

the 3) _____ . The heat and 4) _____ in the mantle cause the rock

to melt into a liquid. This hot melted rock, called 5) _____ , bursts through a

crack in Earth's crust. When the magma flows down the side of the volcano,

we call it 6) _____ . A volcano that has erupted before or that continues

to erupt is called an 7) _____ volcano. Sometimes, when lava cools and

hardens, it plugs up the volcano, and the volcano stops erupting. When this

happens, the volcano is called a sleeping, or 8) _____ , volcano.

Greeting Card Guess

A **simile** is a comparison using the words *like* or *as*.
A **metaphor** is a comparison that does not use *like* or *as*.
The **personification** of a word means giving it human qualities.

Look at each card. Decide if the card's message is an example of simile, metaphor, or personification. Then create your own greeting card using these kinds of **figurative language** to write a message!

1.

Fathers are like coaches. They let you play, but they know when to call a time out!

Happy Father's Day!

This is an example of _____ .

2.

Each year that passes is a new chapter in a book. The older you are, the more pages you have!

Happy Birthday!

This is an example of _____ .

3.

I heard a bossy flu bug moved in with you and makes you stay in bed. There's not much you can do until he bugs someone else instead!

Get Well Soon

This is an example of _____ .

4.

Exactly the Same

Congruent figures are exactly the same shape and size.

Look at each pair of shapes below. Then write **congruent** or **not congruent**.

1.

not congruent

2.

_____

3.

_____

4.

_____

5.

_____

6.

_____

7.

_____

8.

_____

Now, draw a congruent shape to match the shape shown.

9.

10.

Understanding Poetry

Read the following poem by Robert Louis Stevenson.
Then answer the questions.

My Shadow

I have a little shadow that goes in and out with me,
And what can be the use of him is more than I can see.
He is very, very like me from the heels up to the head;
And I see him jump before me, when I jump into my bed.

The funniest thing about him is the way he likes to grow—
Not at all like proper children, which is always very slow;
For he sometimes shoots up taller like an india-rubber ball,
And he sometimes goes so little that there's none of him at all.

He hasn't got a notion of how children ought to play,
And can only make a fool of me in every sort of way.
He stays so close behind me; he's a coward you can see;
I'd think shame to stick to nursie as that shadow sticks to me!

One morning, very early, before the sun was up,
I rose and found the shining dew on every buttercup;
But my lazy little shadow, like an arrant sleepy-head,
Had stayed at home behind me and was fast asleep in bed.

1. What is the rhyming pattern of this poem?

a) aaba aaba   **b)** abcb abcb   **c)** aa bb aa bb

2. What does the child mean when he says his shadow grows in funny ways?

_____

_____

3. Why does the child call his shadow a coward?

_____

_____

4. Write two lines from the poem that give the shadow human qualities.

_____

_____

5. Why does the child call the shadow lazy?

_____

_____

Elevator Out of Order

The story is out of order. Number each group of sentences to show the correct story sequence.

a) _____ By the time she got to the top, she was exhausted. She found her father's office and walked inside. He was so excited to see her.

b) _____ Just as she had finished preparing the dinner, her dad called. He had to work late at his office and he couldn't get home in time for his birthday dinner.

c) _____ "I've come to bring you your birthday dinner," Amy told her dad. "How wonderful," her dad said. "What did you bring?"

d) _____ Amy always did something special for her dad on his birthday. One year, she decided to make her dad a special birthday dinner.

e) _____ When they got to the office building, Amy ran inside with the food packages. She stopped when she saw a big sign on the elevator door. It said, "Elevator Out of Order."

f) _____ Amy and her dad walked down the fourteen flights of stairs. They found the packages of food by the broken elevator.

g) _____ Then Amy had an idea for a birthday surprise. "If Dad can't come to his birthday dinner, then his birthday dinner will go to him!" she told her mom. Amy's mom drove her to his office so that they could drop off the dinner.

h) _____ Amy's father's office was on the fourteenth floor! That's a lot of stairs, but Amy was determined. She started the long trek up the stairs.

i) _____ Just then, her dad's boss approached the elevator. "It looks like the elevator is broken," he said. "You can't walk up fourteen flights of stairs. I guess you can go home for the night!" So Amy, her dad, and the special birthday dinner all went home together.

j) _____ "Oh no!" Amy looked around and couldn't find the packages of food. She realized that she must have left them down by the elevator.

Family Reunion Fun

Follow the directions below.

At the family reunion, 20 people in the family voted on what activities to do. Fill in the blanks to show the percentage of people that voted for each activity.

1. 10 people wanted to go swimming. $\frac{10}{20} = \frac{50}{100} = 50\%$

2. 6 people wanted to go horseback riding. $\frac{6}{20} = \frac{30}{100} =$ _____ %

3. 4 people wanted to go hiking. $\frac{4}{20} = \frac{20}{100} =$ _____ %

4. 2 people wanted to go fishing. $\frac{2}{20} = \frac{10}{100} =$ _____ %

The family reunion lasted for five days, but not everyone could be there every day. This chart shows how many people were there each day.

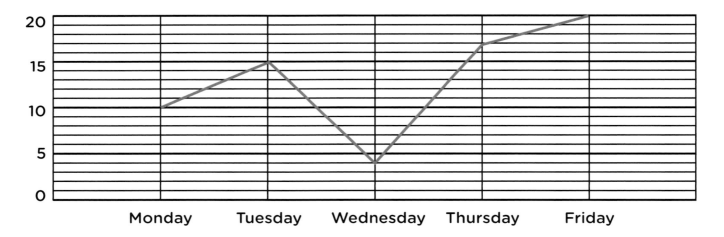

5. On which day were the most people there? _____

6. On which day were the fewest people there? _____

7. How many more people were there on Tuesday than on Monday? _____

8. From which day to which day was there the biggest change in the number of people?

_____ to _____

How Much Is It?

Look at the coins and the bills in each row.
Write the total value of the money.

MONEY	VALUE
1.	$3.10
2.	_____
3.	_____
4.	_____
5.	_____
6.	_____
7.	_____
8.	_____

9. Add #1 and #3 together. What is the total value? _____

10. Add #2 and #6 together. What is the total value? _____

11. Add #4 and #5 together. What is the total value? _____

12. Add #7 and #8 together. What is the total value? _____

Cinquains

A **cinquain** is a five-line poem with a certain number of words or syllables on each line.

Line 1 – The subject (1 word or 2 syllables)
Line 2 – Adjectives (2 words or 4 syllables)
Line 3 – Action verbs (3 words or 6 syllables)
Line 4 – Descriptive phrase (4 to 5 words and 8 syllables)
Line 5 – Synonym or word that sums up the subject (1 word or 2 syllables)

Examples:

Baby	Rain
Soft, cuddly	Fresh, cool
Cooing, gurgling, smiling	Sprinkling, pouring, pattering
Tiny toes and tiny fingers	Wet on my waiting, upturned face
Infant	Shower

Now, write a cinquain of your own, Think of a subject you can describe with vivid adjectives and exciting verbs. Some ideas include sports, friends, weather, school, animals, and food. Use your imagination!

_____

_____ , _____ ,

_____ , _____ , _____ ,

_____

_____

It Takes Coordination

Follow the directions below.

Graph the ordered pairs in the box on the grid. Connect the points as you go. Then connect the first and last point.

| 1,5 | 4,6 | 5,10 | 6,6 | 9,5 | 7,4 | 9,1 | 5,3 | 1,1 | 3,4 |

The ordered pairs on the grid below show the positions of players on a baseball field. Write the coordinates for each position on the chart.

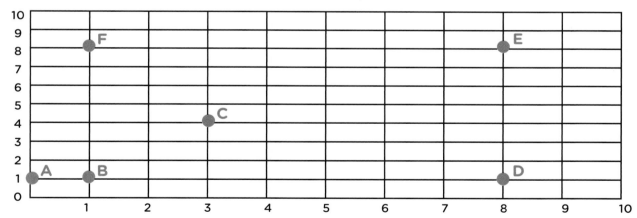

Player	Label	Ordered Pair
Catcher	A	0,1
Batter	B	____
Pitcher	C	____
1st Base	D	____
2nd Base	E	____
3rd Base	F	____

Thomas Jefferson

Read the story. Then fill in the dates and missing information in the time line.

Thomas Jefferson, the third president of the United States, was a politician, patriot, writer, inventor, and builder. As a young boy growing up in Virginia, Thomas had many interests. In 1768, at the young age of 26, he started building a plantation called Monticello. He enjoyed filling his home with his own inventions.

Throughout his life, Thomas Jefferson always fought to protect America's freedom. He was at the second Continental Congress in 1776, where he was asked to write the Declaration of Independence. This important document was the beginning of the Revolutionary War.

Jefferson went on to serve the country in many ways. As a member of Congress in 1783, he helped create the American money system. Then, from 1796 to 1801, he was vice president to John Adams. In 1801, Thomas Jefferson was elected president. In 1803, he bought an important piece of land from France. This is known as the Louisiana Purchase.

In 1809, Jefferson retired and returned to Monticello, but even after retiring, he continued to help his country. In 1819, he founded and built the University of Virginia. By the end of his life, Jefferson had spent more than fifty years serving his country!

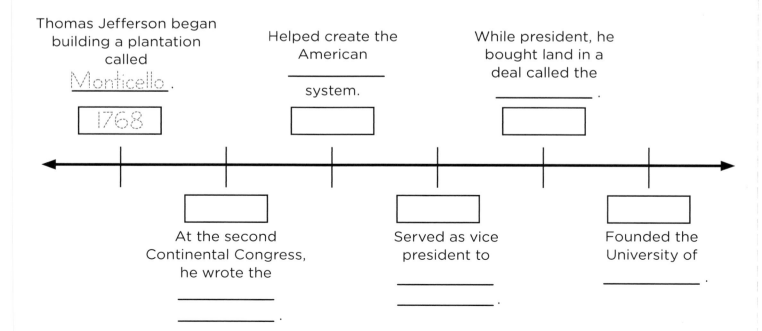

Thomas Jefferson began building a plantation called
Monticello.

1768

At the second Continental Congress, he wrote the _____ .

Helped create the American _____ system.

Served as vice president to _____ .

While president, he bought land in a deal called the _____ .

Founded the University of _____ .

Division Search

There are 20 division problems in this puzzle. Circle each problem.
Hints: Problems can go across or down. A number
can be used in more than one problem.

6	25	5	5	12	16	2	8
3	40	9	5	20	8	4	2
24	8	3	1	10	2	30	4
15	5	3	13	2	36	6	6
30	11	7	28	5	60	5	12
14	32	55	7	40	10	4	4
2	9	11	4	18	6	12	3
7	4	5	0	5	21	8	2

Creative Comparisons

Follow the directions below.

A **simile** is a comparison using the words *like* or *as*.

Tara's smile was as bright as a ray of sunshine.

A **metaphor** is a direct comparison without using the words *like* or *as*.

The tornado was a monster ripping through the town.

Complete each sentence by writing a simile. Use vivid words for your comparison.

1. Dad's voice boomed like a _____ .

2. As fluffy as _____ , the clouds floated in the sky.

3. The stars twinkled like _____ on the velvet black night sky.

4. The baby chick felt as soft as _____ against my skin.

5. Nora's hair is as red as _____ .

Complete each sentence by writing a metaphor. Use vivid words for your comparisons.

6. Brian Picket was a _____ on the football field.

7. The fans were _____ , exploding into cheers when their team scored.

8. Emily is a shy little _____ , hiding her face in her mom's skirts.

9. Hunting slyly in the grass, my cat Chester is a _____ .

10. The ocean is a _____ , holding me in its cool welcoming arms.

Write two similes and metaphors of your own.

11. best friend _____ Compared to _____

12. new teacher _____ Compared to _____

13. fast car _____ Compared to _____

14. fluffy kitten _____ Compared to _____

Crossword Puzzle

Erosion is the process by which material is worn away.
Each word in the puzzle is related to erosion. Use the clues to complete the puzzle.

1. a v a l a n c h e

Across
1. A landslide of snow moving quickly down a mountain side
2. A large body of ice that slowly moves, taking pieces of land along with it
3. The force that pulls everything downward, causing rain and soil to run down a slope

Down
1. Polluted rainwater that can burn plants and corrode rocks
4. A sudden rush of mud and debris falling down a slope
5. The wearing down of rocks, soil, or land by nature's forces
6. Small particles, like dirt, that can be scattered by wind and water
7. Hard, solid masses that can be worn down by wind and water

Sally's Scenes

Setting is the time and place in which something happens. **Mood** is the feeling or emotion in a story. Read each sentence and write a word to describe the setting. Then choose the word that best describes the mood.

Mood Words

happy	serious
frightening	hopeful

1. Sally had lost control of her bike! She gripped the handlebars tightly as the bike sped downhill toward Mrs. Grady's house. Sally screamed and shut her eyes as her bike crashed into Mrs. Grady's fence. She flew off her bike and landed by the flower pots. One of the pots broke into pieces and the plants were crushed.

Setting: _Mrs. Grady's house_
Mood: _frightening_

2. The hospital room was cold and gray. Sally lay on the stiff exam table while the doctor bandaged her aching foot. Sally's mom sat next to her, looking worried.

"One of Mrs. Grady's flower pots was destroyed," her mom said. "We'll need to replace it for her."

Setting: _____
Mood: _____

3. When Sally woke up the next morning, her foot was feeling a little better. Mrs. Grady's flower pot was in her bedroom, and the pieces had been glued back together. The plant was still damaged, but the leaves were perking back up.

"Mrs. Grady and I repaired the pot," Sally's mom said. "It's almost as good as new!"

Setting: _____
Mood: _____

4. Sally still couldn't walk, but she could sit in the sunshine and help Mrs. Grady with her blooming garden. The pot was back in one piece, and the plant was strong and healthy again. Sally had a healthy glow on her face, too.

"All it takes is a little care and some sunshine to make something as good as new," Mrs. Grady said with a smile.

Setting: _____
Mood: _____

Standard and Expanded Numbers

Numbers can be written in standard or expanded form.

1. 90,925 = 90,000 + 0 + 900 + 20 + 5

2. 43,602 =

3. 794,833 =

4. 277,518 =

5. 1,355,674 =

6. 80,000 + 3,000 + 900 + 70 + 2 =

7. 50,000 + 1,000 + 800 + 80 + 5 =

8. 600,000 + 60,000 + 2,000 + 0 + 90 + 3 =

9. 300,000 + 10,000 + 7,000 + 500 + 40 + 5 =

10. 2,000,000 + 700,000 + 20,000 + 5,000 + 500 + 90 + 8 =

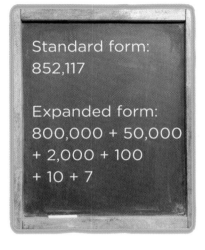

Standard form:
852,117

Expanded form:
800,000 + 50,000
+ 2,000 + 100
+ 10 + 7

11. 798,442 =

_____ hundred thousands   _____ ten thousands   _____ thousands

_____ hundreds   _____ tens   _____ ones

12. 6,991,725 =

_____ millions   _____ hundred thousands   _____ ten thousands

_____ thousands   _____ hundreds   _____ tens

_____ ones

The Need to Agree

Read the following passage about ferrets. Then go back to each sentence. If the subject and the verb agree, write **yes** on the line. If the subject and the verb do not agree, rewrite the verb on the line so that it agrees with the subject.

1. Ferrets makes great pets! **2.** At the beginning of the year, my fifth grade class adopted a ferret as our class pet. **3.** We named him Charlie. **4.** Charlie love to play with us all day long. **5.** Ms. Gomez told us that ferrets is very smart animals. **6.** They learn new tricks very quickly. **7.** He jump through hoops. **8.** He also beg for food and runs through a maze to find treats. **9.** We trained him to use a litter box, just like a cat! **10.** Each day, someone in the class take Charlie for a walk. **11.** We knows that ferrets need a lot of exercise. **12.** He have a special harness and leash. **13.** Charlie loves to go outside, but we need to be careful. **14.** We don't ever wants him to get loose or lost. **15.** When we're in the classroom, Charlie like to chatter at us from his cage. **16.** This often gets the whole class laughing. **17.** He is also very cuddly. **18.** Sometimes he fall asleep right in my arms.

1. _____make_____   2. _____

3. _____   4. _____

5. _____   6. _____

7. _____   8. _____

9. _____   10. _____

11. _____   12. _____

13. _____   14. _____

15. _____   16. _____

17. _____   18. _____

Mr. Fix It

There is one mistake in each sentence. Find the mistakes and rewrite the correct paragraph on a separate sheet of paper.

Look for sentences that need commas or punctuation at the end of the sentence. Check to make sure words are capitalized. Find words that need apostrophes. Check verbs for the correct tense and subject/verb agreement.

1) this summer, my dad wanted to fix up our house. **2)** He reads an article in *home improvement* magazine about how to do repairs. **3)** We didnt have many tools at our house. **4)** My dad had a saw a hammer and some nails. **5)** We tried to do the repairs, but my dads tools were too old. **6)** We werent able to fix anything correctly. **7)** So I decided it were time to ask for some help. **8)** I looked through the chicago gazette for an advertisement. **9)** I saw an ad for a man named Mr. Fix It, so I writed him a letter. **10)** I asked him to come to 355 mulberry street and help us with our repairs. **11)** A few days later mr. Fix It showed up at our house. **12)** He new how to do just about everything. **13)** He have all kinds of great tools, so the job was fast and easy. **14)** What would we have done without Mr. Fix It **15)** Within a few day's, everything was fixed. **16)** The only problem was that my dad's old tools was all broken!

What Fraction Is It?

Write the fraction for each set of shaded shapes. Then reduce the fraction.

1.

$$\frac{8}{10} = \frac{4}{5}$$

2.  ___ = ___

3.  ___ = ___

4.  ___ = ___

5.  ___ = ___

6.  ___ = ___

7.  ___ = ___

8.  ___ = ___

9.  ___ = ___

10. 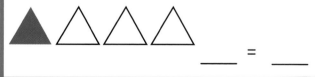  ___ = ___

Pick the Pronoun

Write the correct **pronoun** for each word or words in bold.
Here are some common pronouns and possessive pronouns.

I, me, my, mine	we, us, our, ours	he, him, his
she, her, hers	it, its	they, them, their theirs

Two elephants escaped the city zoo this morning! As **the elephants** ran down Main Street, people fled in fear. "Why are you afraid of **the elephants**?" a young girl asked. **The girl** came up with a quick solution. **The girl** laid a trail of peanuts all the way back to the zoo. The elephants followed **the girl's** peanut trail without a struggle. Now the elephants are back in **the elephants'** home, safe and sound.

1. <u>they</u>   2. _____   3. _____

4. _____   5. _____   6. _____

Miguel had a fantastic birthday party. **Miguel** invited all his friends from class. **Miguel and his friends** had a great time! First was the arcade. Kim was the best at video games. **Kim** even won a baseball cap. Kim gave **the baseball cap** to Miguel as a gift. Next, the kids ordered some pizza. **The pizza** was delicious, but it left **the kids** wanting more. Next stop, ice cream!

7. _____   8. _____   9. _____

10. _____   11. _____   12. _____

Jing Mae and her family came all the way to the United States from China. **Jing Mae and her family** wanted to join other relatives who had moved years earlier. Jing Mae gave **myself** a doll from China. **The doll** is made from fragile painted glass. Jing Mae and **myself** have become best friends. **Jing Mae and I** share all of **Jing Mae and my** most secret hopes and dreams for the future.

13. _____   14. _____   15. _____

16. _____   17. _____   18. _____

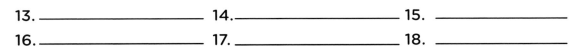

Favorite Foods

This pie chart shows kids' favorite snacks at the Snack Shack.

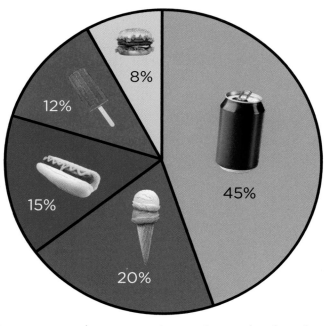

To change a percentage to a decimal, set the decimal point two numbers from the right.
55% = 55. = .55

Change each percentage to a decimal.

1. 45% % = .45

2. _____ % = _____

3. _____ % = _____

4. _____ % = _____

5. _____ % = _____

20 kids were asked about their favorite snack. 45% said it was soda. How many kids is 45% of 20?
45% = .45

```
   20
 × .45
  100
  800
 9.00  ──────▶ remember to set decimal point
```

9 kids said soda was their favorite snack.

6. 20% of 20 kids said ice cream was their favorite snack. How many kids is that?

_____ kids

```
   20
 × .20
```

The Importance of Order

Events in a story must be told in **sequence**, or in the correct order, to make sense. Read the following passage. Then answer the questions.

Today my grandpa taught me how to make ham and cheese pie. First, you have to gather the ingredients: 1 cup of ham cut into chunks, $\frac{1}{2}$ cup shredded cheddar or mozzarella cheese, 4 eggs, 2 cups of light cream, a pinch of salt, and a pinch of pepper. Then preheat the oven to 375°F. Grease the bottom of a large pie plate. Then scatter the ham to cover the bottom of the plate. Sprinkle the cheese over the ham. Mix together the eggs, cream, salt, and pepper. Pour the mixture over the cheese and ham. Bake the cheese pie for about 40 minutes. Test the pie for doneness by inserting a knife in the middle. If the knife comes out clean, the pie is done. Let the pie cool for at least 10 minutes before serving.

1. What is the first step in making ham and cheese pie?

_____

2. What is the last step in making ham and cheese pie?

_____

3. What do you do right before putting the ham in the pie plate?

_____

4. What do you do right after baking the pie for 40 minutes?

_____

5. Would it matter if these steps were written in a different order? Why or why not?

_____

_____

6. On the lines below, write steps telling someone how to do or make something. Number your steps in order.

_____

_____

_____

_____

_____

Fun in the Sun

Read the passages and follow the directions below.

Passage A

Don't get burned! A sunburn can make you miss out on summer vacation. That's why you need Super Summer Sunscreen. It lasts for a really long time, and it doesn't wash off in the water. So you can spend all day splashing around with your friends and never get burned. If you want to have a super summer, tell your parents to buy Super Summer Sunscreen for you!

Passage B

It's important to keep your kids safe from the sun during the summer. The sun's rays can cause damage to the skin and leave a painful sunburn. Here are some tips to prevent your kids from getting burned this summer.

- Make sure they put on sunscreen every day.
- Have them wear a hat or visor and sunglasses.
- The sun's rays are most damaging between 10:00 AM and 2:00 PM, so be extra careful during this time.

Read each phrase and decide if it describes passage A or B. Put a check in the correct column.

	A	B
1. An advertisement	✓	
2. An informative paragraph with tips		
3. Wants to inform the reader about preventing sunburn		
4. Wants the reader to buy a certain sunscreen		
5. Aimed at kids		
6. Aimed at parents		

Factors of Numbers

A **factor** is a number that divides into another number.
Circle the factors for each number. Write the number of factors you circled in the box.

1. 144
(12, 6, 1,) 9, 10

[3]   O

2. 20
10, 4, 5, 2, 1, 20, 15

[ ]   S

3. 14
7, 8, 10, 3, 6

[ ]   E

4. 36
6, 9, 4, 12, 7, 3

[ ]   P

5. 56
16, 12, 10, 9, 5, 18

[ ]   A

6. 100
25, 9, 2, 100, 50, 12, 10, 5, 20

[ ]   R

7. 18
9, 5, 6, 3, 18, 4, 10

[ ]   M

8. 48
8, 10, 4, 15, 5, 9

[ ]   I

To solve the riddle, write the letter that goes with each answer on the line.

Riddle: You can keep it only after giving it away to someone else. What is it?

Answer:

____ ____ ____ ____ ____ ____ ____ ____
 0   5   7   3   4   2   6   1

Fill in the missing factors for each number.

9. 16
8, _____, _____, 4, _____

10. 12
_____, _____, 12, 1, _____, 3

11. 28
14, _____, _____, _____, 28, _____

12. 30
_____, 3, _____, _____, _____, 5, 15, _____

Adverb Action

An **adverb** is a word that tells more about a verb. It tells **how**, **when**, or **where** an action is done.

> **Example:**
> How: quickly, silently   When: today, always   Where: outside, there

Use the clues and the adverbs in the box to complete the crossword puzzle.

Adverbs
fondly	carefully
suddenly	soon
here	quietly
inside	anywhere
early	loudly
weekly	extremely

Across

4. Don't worry; your mom will be here _____ .

5. The train left _____ so we were stranded at the station.

7. Our city newspaper is delivered on a _____ basis.

9. Please tiptoe _____ past the sleeping baby's room.

11. Joel is _____ happy about winning the spelling bee.

12. I _____ remember carefree summer days at the beach.

Down

1. The dog _____ jumped up and barked, scaring the child.

2. The kittens are playing _____ the box.

3. We can eat _____ you want, as long as it's not pizza again!

6. Children laughed _____ as the monkey did tricks.

8. Handle that pot _____ , as it is very hot.

10. You can leave your coat right _____ on the bed.

The Quote Boat

Read the passage below and add quotation marks
to the sentences that need them.

Put quotations around:
A speaker's words:
"Let's go sailing," Sam said.
Titles of magazine articles, songs,
and poems:
Pam reads "Sail Away" in *Sailing*
magazine

Pam and Sam liked to go sailing. One day they took their sailboat out on the water, but there was no wind to push the sail.

Oh no! said Pam. We'll never be able to sail without some wind.

We just need to be patient and wait for the wind, Sam said.

So Pam and Sam waited and waited. When there was still no wind, Pam said, We can't wait around all day. We need to do something.

What can we do? Sam asked. We can't control the wind!

Let's close our eyes and think about the wind, Pam said. Think of the windiest day you can remember.

Okay, Sam said. Sam remembered a storm that was so windy, a tree in front of his house blew over. He closed his eyes and thought about that very windy day.

Pretty soon, the sky started to get dark. It was getting windy.

Pam shouted, Hooray! Now we can go sailing.

Just then it got windier and it started to rain. The wind even blew Pam's copies of the Sail Away article from *Sailing* magazine out of the boat. Both Pam and Sam knew it was too dangerous to sail in this weather.

Gee, Sam, Pam said. You didn't have to think that hard!

Multiplying with Decimals

Complete each problem by filling in the answers.

Multiply by	Move the Decimal Point	Example
10	1 place to the right	10 × 5.17 = 51.7
100	2 places to the right	100 × 5.17 = 517
1,000	3 places to the right	1,000 × 5.17 = 5,170

1. Multiply by 10

Input	Output
2.05	20.5
0.94	9.4
25.42	254.2
7.48	74.8

2. Multiply by 100

Input	Output
.430	
1.86	
50.09	
.033	

3. Multiply by 1,000

Input	Output
16.3	
.089	
8.51	
0.726	

4. Multiply by 10

Input	Output
3.905	
0.008	
19.4	
90.76	

5. Multiply by 100

Input	Output
0.001	
7.82	
0.292	
84.19	

6. Multiply by 1,000

Input	Output
0.36	
1.39	
100.1	
78.05	

7. Multiply by 10

Input	Output
0.15	
27.18	
8.661	
.907	

8. Multiply by 100

Input	Output
0.355	
7.22	
81.01	
0.909	

9. Multiply by 1,000

Input	Output
545.01	
.180	
.014	
43.00	

Movie Mania

You have been chosen to review a movie in your local newspaper.
What movie would you like to review? You can
choose a movie you liked or disliked. Include the following in your review:

- Title of movie
- Main characters
- Summary of plot
- Reasons why you liked or disliked the movie
- Examples supporting your reasons

Example:

Wild Waters was the most interesting movie I've seen all year. The film follows surfing superstar Kelli Thomas on her climb to the world championships in Hawaii. We see Kelli struggle with training and even deal with a devastating injury. The camera work was really exciting! Cameras were strapped to Kelli's surfboard and her arm. The shots were incredible! You felt like you were speeding through the waves along with her. The movie did a great job of showing Kelli's climb from junior competitions all the way to the top. It also showed how hard someone has to work to make it in the surfing world. I would highly recommend this movie to anyone who loves surfing or just wants to take a wild ride through a great story!

_____
_____
_____
_____
_____
_____
_____
_____
_____
_____
_____
_____
_____

The Crossing of Columbus

There are four false statements about Columbus in the boxes below. Cross out each box that has a false statement. Look at an encyclopedia if you need help.

1. King Ferdinand and Queen Isabella of Spain funded Columbus's voyage.	**2.** Columbus, like most people of his time, believed that the world was flat.	**3.** On his return voyage to Spain, Columbus brought back some of his discoveries, including pineapple, tobacco, and Native Americans.
4. On his first voyage, Columbus wanted to find a shortcut to India by sailing west instead of east.	**5.** The ships of his first voyage were named the *Niña*, *Pinta*, and *Santa Maria*.	**6.** Even up to his death, Columbus believed that he had reached Asia and India on his voyages.
7. Women were not allowed on any of Columbus's voyages.	**8.** Columbus believed that the ships of his first voyage had brought him good luck, so he used the same ships for all four of his voyages.	**9.** Columbus was the first European to explore North America and the United States.

4 x 4 Magic Squares

All rows and columns in these "magic" squares add up to the magic number. Can you complete the magic squares? Hint: You can only use a number once!

1. All rows and columns add up to 30.

		2	15
3	14		4
	0	7	
	11		1

2. All rows and columns add up to 34.

16		3	9
5	15		
	1		14
2		13	

3. All rows and columns add up to 37.

	6	9	
10		4	
8	1	17	
	12		2

4. All rows and columns add up to 40.

	7		19
5	18	11	
17			12
8		16	

5. All rows and columns add up to 45.

11		5	
	20	12	
19	3		13
			4

Showing Possession

A **possessive** noun shows possession or ownership.

- For a possessive singular noun, add an **apostrophe** and *s* (sled's).
- For a possessive plural noun, add an **apostrophe** (sleds').
- For a possessive irregular plural noun, add an **apostrophe** and *s* (men's).

Circle the correct possessive or plural noun to complete the sentence.

1. This _____ bone is buried in the yard.	dogs' M	(dog's) C	dogs R
2. Those _____ toys are in the closet.	childrens' O	childrens L	children's H
3. _____ shoes are on sale this weekend.	Women's I	Womens A	Womens' T
4. Did you hear those _____ giggles?	babies' C	babies W	babies's E
5. Four _____ tails are more than eight inches.	rats S	rat's Y	rats' K
6. The _____ soccer season starts next week.	girl's U	girls' I	girls F
7. We watched _____ playing in the field.	horses N	horse's G	horses' P
8. Are these your _____ backpacks?	students' A	student's D	students E
9. Unpack those _____ contents in the garage.	boxes's R	boxes T	boxes' N
10. My _____ flower garden is in bloom.	grandmas O	grandma's E	grandmas' H
11. Those _____ beds are soft and fuzzy.	puppies W	puppies' G	puppies's U
12. How many _____ will be coming to lunch?	ladies's S	ladies' Y	ladies G

To solve the riddle, write the letters under the nouns you circled in order on the lines.

Riddle: I live in a little house all alone. My house has no doors or windows. If I want to get out, I must break through a wall. What am I?

Answer: A ___ ___ ___ ___ ___   ___ ___   ___ ___ ___

Scrambled Systems

Unscramble the letters to name each system of the body.

1. This system circulates blood, oxygen, and nutrients through the body.

    Y R C L U I A T C O R ___circulatory___

2. This system deals with breathing.

    S O E I R P T R Y A R _____

3. This system of nerves allows the brain to send messages to other parts of the body.

    V U R N E O S _____

4. This system digests and breaks down the food we eat.

    G T S E V I D E I _____

5. This system attacks germs and fights off infections.

    M U N M I E _____

6. This system includes 206 bones that make up our skeleton.

    L K E E T S A L _____

7. This system includes more than 640 muscles that allow us to move.

    R U C M L U A S _____

8. This system helps circulate fluids and keeps disease out of the body.

    A L M P H C Y T I _____

Camping Conflict

Read the passage and follow the directions below.

Robin and Katie were so excited when their parents announced that the family was going on a summer camping trip. Both sisters loved being outdoors.

"All we need to do is decide what kind of campsite we want to go to, and then we can start planning," their dad said.

"Let's go camping by a lake," said Robin. "I really want to go swimming!"

"We can swim at the pool any time," said Katie. "Let's camp in the desert where I can go rock climbing."

"No way," said Robin. "The desert is too hot, and I don't know how to rock climb."

The sisters were angry with each other, and they couldn't agree on a place for the family to camp. They argued all through dinner. Then their mom had an idea.

"Why don't we go camping at the beach?" she suggested. "Robin, you can swim in the ocean water. There are lots of rocks by the tide pools that Katie can explore."

"I don't know if I'd like swimming in salt water," said Robin.

"Rock climbing by the beach isn't the same as in the desert," Katie pointed out.

"It may not be exactly what you had in mind," Dad said, "But the beach is a good compromise. Both of you get to do what you want."

The girls finally agreed to go camping at the beach. Robin found that she enjoyed swimming in the ocean even more than in a lake. Katie had a great time climbing all the rocks by the water. Plus, the sisters discovered something that they both enjoyed equally. They liked building sand castles!

The **conflict** of a story is the main problem. The solution to that problem is called the **resolution**. Describe the conflict and the resolution of the story on the lines below.

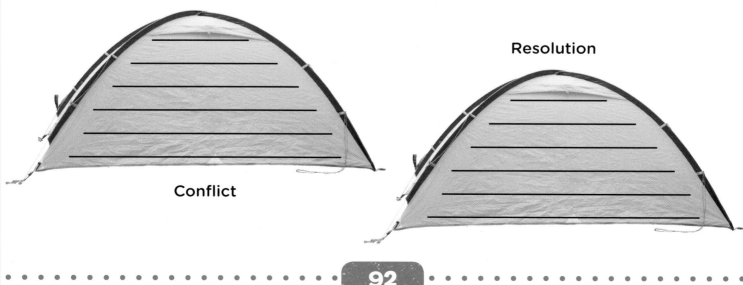

Resolution

Conflict

So Many Choices!

Salad Station has a huge salad bar with many different choices. The choices to go with each salad are tomatoes, olives, cheese, mushrooms, bacon, chicken, onions, egg, broccoli, and sprouts.

How many different combinations can you make? List them below, only once for each combination.

Tomatoes

olives
cheese
mushrooms
bacon
chicken
onions
egg
broccoli
sprouts

Olives

_____
_____
_____
_____
_____
_____
_____
_____

Cheese

_____
_____
_____
_____
_____
_____

Mushrooms

_____
_____
_____
_____
_____

Bacon

_____
_____
_____
_____

Chicken

_____
_____
_____
_____

Onions

_____
_____
_____

Egg

_____
_____

Broccoli

_____

Good Descriptions

Adjectives describe nouns or pronouns. An adjective tells how many, what kind, or which one. Write three descriptive adjectives for each noun. Use interesting, specific words that tell how something looks, smells, sounds, feels, tastes, or acts.

Examples:
<u>Two</u> rabbits.   <u>Two</u> <u>fuzzy</u> rabbits.   <u>Two</u> of <u>those</u> <u>fuzzy</u> rabbits.

1. Baby
_____
_____
_____

2. Ice cream
_____
_____
_____

3. Rose
_____
_____
_____

4. Car
_____
_____
_____

5. Winter
_____
_____
_____

6. Puppy
_____
_____
_____

7. Dinosaur
_____
_____
_____

8. Clouds
_____
_____
_____

9. Beach
_____
_____
_____

Choose four nouns you described above. Write a sentence using each noun and at least two of your descriptive adjectives.

10. _____

11. _____

12. _____

13. _____

Picture This

Follow the directions below.

> A **fact** is something that we know for sure.
> An **inference** is an educated guess based on clues.

Look at the picture below. Check off whether each statement is a fact or an inference about what you see in the picture.

	Fact	Inference
1. The boy hurt his knee.	√	
2. The boy fell.		
3. The boy has scratches on his knee.		
4. The boy is in a lot of pain.		
5. The boy isn't wearing a helmet.		
6. He is bleeding.		
7. The boy was riding his skateboard too fast.		
8. The wet pavement caused the boy to fall of his skateboard.		
9. The boy will get a bandage for his knee.		
10. The boy feels upset about falling down.		

Average Avenue

There are three kinds of averages: the **mode**, the **median**, and the **mean**.

The **mode** is the number that occurs most often.
2, **5**, 3, 8, **5**, 2, **5**
The mode is 5.

Find the mode in each set of numbers.

1. 14, 7, 3, 14, 12, 7, 14 _____

2. 45, 26, 28, 32, 26, 32, 26 _____

3. 3, -2, 1, -2, -1, -3 _____

The **median** is the middle number in an ordered list of numbers.
4, 7, 12, 5, 8
First, order the numbers from least to greatest.
4, 5, **7**, 8, 12
The median is 7.

Find the median in each set of numbers.

4. 12, 5, 7, 10, 13 _____

5. 3, 15, 2, 9, 6, 11, 12 _____

6. -3, 2, 1, -2, 4 _____

To find the **mean**, add all the numbers together. Then divide that sum by the total number of addends.
3, 9, 4, 3, 6
3 + 9 + 4 + 3 + 6 = 25
There are 5 addends in the list. 25 divided by 5 = 5.
The mean is 5.

Find the mean for each list of numbers.

7. 5, 1, 4, 2

8. 7, 8, 5, 4

9. 2, 4, 6, 1, 2

Searching for Clues

When you are reading, you can use context clues to figure out unfamiliar words. **Context clues** are the words around the unfamiliar word that help you understand what you're reading. Read the following passage. Then answer the questions.

Chelsey comes from a daring family. They seem to have no fear and have lived very adventurous lives. Her grandma May flew warplanes in World War II. She has many thrilling stories to tell. Her father, Brent, was a stuntman in the movies. He jumped out of windows, sometimes hurtling ten long stories to the ground. He also rolled and crashed cars. Chelsey's mother owns a skydiving business. So far, her mom has completed 48 jumps. Most of the time her mom jumps in tandem with first-time clients to make sure everything goes smoothly. For beginners, this is much safer than jumping solo. Chelsey is proud of her adventurous family. She is a daredevil in her own right! She has been freestyle skiing for six years. When she sails off the jumps, twisting and turning, she never fails to dazzle the cheering crowd. Chelsey hopes she will make the Olympic team someday.

1. What does the word **daring** mean? How do you know?

_____

_____

2. What does the word **hurtling** mean? What context clues helped you figure out the meaning of the word?

_____

_____

3. Why would jumping **solo** be unsafe for beginning skydivers?

_____

_____

4. What does the word **dazzle** mean? How do you know?

_____

_____

5. Write a sentence using the word **daring**.

_____

6. Write a sentence using the word **dazzle**.

_____

Add It Up

You can add negative numbers together. If both numbers are negative, just add the numbers together and keep the negative sign.

Solve the problems by adding two negative numbers together.

$$2 + 2 = 4 \qquad -2 + -2 = -4$$

1. The elevator went down 1 floor. Then it went down 2 more floors. How many floors down is it now?

-1 + -2 = -3

2. The elevator was 2 floors below the ground. It went down 3 more floors.

-2 + -3 = _____

3. The elevator went down 5 floors. Then it went down 1 more floor.

-5 + -1 = _____

4. The elevator started out 3 floors below the ground. Then it went down 6 more floors.

-3 + _____ = _____

5. The elevator went down 4 floors. Then it went down 4 more floors.

_____ + _____ = _____

6. -6 + -2 = _____

7. -5 + -4 = _____

8. -8 + -1 = _____

9. -3 + -4 = _____

10. -2 + -9 = _____

Chief John Ross

Read the passage and answer the questions below.

One of the most important Native American leaders in American history didn't look like a Native American at all. His name was John Ross, and he had Cherokee ancestors that made him one-eighth Cherokee. He helped fight for the rights of the Cherokee. In 1817, Ross was elected to the Cherokee National Council. He became president of the council from 1819 to 1826.

Ross fought for the Cherokee with words instead of weapons. He wrote a constitution for the Cherokee people and was elected principal chief in 1828. They became the first Indian Republic. Ross's hope was that a star would be added to the US flag to represent the Cherokee Nation.

Despite Ross's efforts, the Cherokee were still forced off their land. In 1838, John Ross had to lead his people from Georgia to Oklahoma. Thousands died on this journey, and it became known as the Trail of Tears. Even John Ross's wife died on the trek.

Once in Oklahoma, John Ross continued to serve as principal chief of the Cherokee Nation until his death in 1866. He died in Washington, D.C., where he had been working on a treaty between the Cherokee and the U.S. government.

Use context clues to connect each word with its meaning.

1. ancestor
2. elect
3. council
4. republic
5. treaty

a) to choose someone to be a leader
b) an agreement between two parties
c) a nation in which people elect their leaders
d) family relatives that lived in the past
e) a group of leaders that work together

6. Number the events to put them in the correct sequence.

_____ John Ross served as principal chief in Oklahoma.

_____ When the Cherokee were forced off their land, Ross led them from Georgia to Oklahoma on the Trail of Tears.

_____ John Ross served on the Cherokee National Council and became president.

_____ The Cherokee became the first Indian Republic and John Ross was elected the principal chief.

_____ In Washington, D.C., John Ross worked on a treaty between the Cherokee and the U.S. government.

Reading between the Lines

The owners of Mimi's Muffins keep track of how many muffins they sell per week. Using a line graph helps them see how the business is doing. Look at the data in the line graph. It shows changes over time. Read the graph. Then answer the questions.

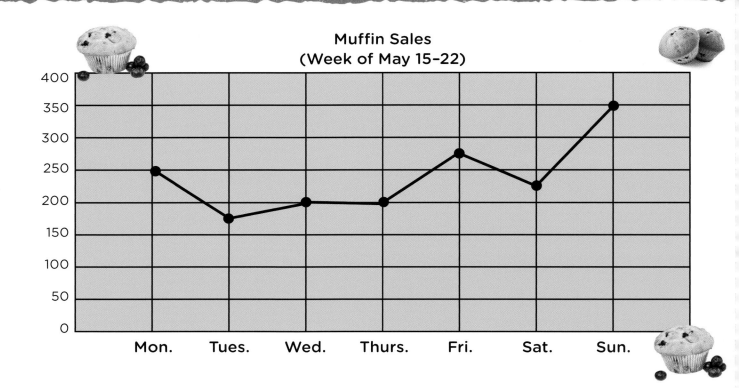

1. How many muffins were sold on Tuesday? _____175_____

2. How many muffins were sold on Saturday? _____

3. How many more muffins were sold on Friday than on Monday? _____

4. On which two days were muffin sales the same? _____ and _____

5. Last week, Mimi's Muffins sold 1,600 muffins. Did sales rise or fall this week?

_____

6. How many more muffins were sold on the highest day than on the lowest day?

_____

Alike and Opposite

Synonyms are words that mean the same as other words.

Antonyms are words with the opposite meaning as other words.

Look at sentences 1–6 and choose the word that means the same thing as the underlined word. Then, in sentences 7–12, choose the word that means the opposite of the underlined word.

1. The runner felt weak and <u>tired</u>.
a) exhausted
b) bored
c) amazed
d) surprised

2. The <u>shy</u> mouse hid under the couch.
a) funny
b) friendly
c) timid
d) silly

3. Melissa <u>paused</u> before her speech.
a) wondered
b) hesitated
c) thought
d) stood

4. The carnival ride was <u>frightening</u>.
a) horrible
b) confusing
c) dangerous
d) terrifying

5. "Did you like the book?" Lin <u>questioned</u>.
a) inquired
b) stated
c) demanded
d) suggested

6. He often came across as <u>conceited</u>.
a) evil
b) arrogant
c) noble
d) intelligent

7. Juvia's plane <u>departs</u> at noon.
a) leaves
b) lands
c) arrives
d) goes

8. Dad will <u>repair</u> Eric's car.
a) crash
b) destroy
c) steal
d) fix

9. Tanya hoped the scar was <u>temporary</u>.
a) visible
b) dreadful
c) modest
d) permanent

10. Mario was <u>pleased</u> with his grades.
a) disappointed
b) interested
c) happy
d) insulted

11. Dr. Greer is <u>generous</u> with his patients.
a) giving
b) stingy
c) random
d) disturbing

12. The song will <u>precede</u> the dance.
a) shorten
b) complete
c) pass
d) follow

Reading Road Trip

Figure out the part of speech for each bold word.
Write the word under the correct heading below.

Noun: a person, place, or thing
> *sister, kitchen, chair*

Proper noun: a person, place, or thing with a specific name
> *Susan, Disneyland, Rocky Mountains*

Verb: an action word
> *is, go, visit*

Verb phrase: two or more words working together to express the action
> *should be, will go, can visit*

Reggie Roberts was not excited about the two-week road trip his family had planned for the **summer**.

"We **should go** to Hawaii instead," said Reggie.

"I promise you **will have** a good time," his mom said.

The Roberts family left their home in Denver, **Colorado**, and drove for two days until they **reached** Yellowstone National Park in Wyoming. They camped inside the park and visited a **geyser** named Old Faithful. **Reggie** was amazed as he watched tons of water shoot up out of a hole in the ground.

After staying at **Yellowstone** for a few days, they **packed** up their car again. They had to drive for three days to reach the Black Hills of South Dakota. Reggie's family visited a place called **Mount Rushmore**. Reggie **could hardly believe** that the faces of four **presidents** are actually carved into rock! A tour guide **told** him that each face is more than 60 feet high, and the whole monument took fourteen years to carve.

It **took** three more days for the family to drive back to Colorado. Reggie passed the time by reading some books he **had bought** about Mount Rushmore and watching the scenery. He was glad they had gone on the trip.

"It was a long **drive**," he said, "but it was worth it!"

Noun	Proper Noun	Verb	Verb Phrase
_____	_____	_____	_____
_____	_____	_____	_____
_____	_____	_____	_____
_____	_____	_____	_____

Rooms in the House

Perimeter is the sum of the length of all of a shape's sides. To get the perimeter of a room, add all the sides together. **Area** is the amount of space a shape covers. To get the area of a room, multiply the length times the width (l × w).

Find the perimeter of each room.

1.

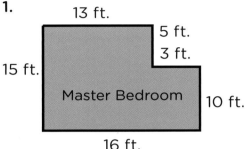

13 ft.

5 ft.

3 ft.

15 ft.

Master Bedroom

10 ft.

16 ft.

Perimeter = ___62 ft___

2.

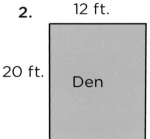

12 ft.

20 ft.

Den

Perimeter = _____

3.

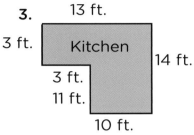

13 ft.

3 ft.

Kitchen

14 ft.

3 ft.

11 ft.

10 ft.

Perimeter = _____

Now find the area of the shaded part of each room. Write your answers in square feet (sq. ft.)

4.

Bathroom 1

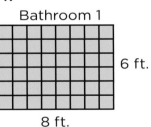

6 ft.

8 ft.

Area = _____

5.

Garage

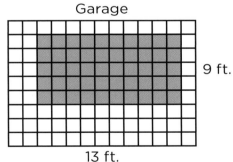

9 ft.

13 ft.

Area = _____

6.

Bedroom 1

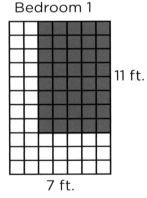

11 ft.

7 ft.

Area = _____

7.

Family Room

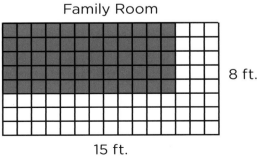

8 ft.

15 ft.

Area = _____

8. What is the total perimeter of all the rooms put together?

Perimeter = _____

9. What is the total area of Bathroom 1, the Garage, Bedroom 1, and the Family Room?

Area = _____

Nouns in Analogies

Complete these analogies with nouns. Remember, think of how the words in the first set relate to each other.

An **analogy** shows a relationship between two words or ideas.
For example: *Lamb is to ewe as kitten is to* _____ .
To complete the analogy, you need to figure out the relationship of a lamb to ewe. A ewe is a lamb's mother. So, the missing word should be a kitten's mother, or cat.

1. Milk is to cow as egg is to __chicken__ .

2. Thermometer is to temperature as ruler is to _____ .

3. Mouse is to mice as tooth is to _____ .

4. Shark is to fish as snake is to _____ .

5. Earth is to planet as sun is to _____ .

6. Earthquake is to earth as tidal wave is to _____ .

7. Shelf is to shelves as calf is to _____ .

8. Claws are to paw as fingernails are to _____ .

9. Pacific is to ocean as Mississippi is to _____ .

10. Atlas is to maps as dictionary is to _____ .

11. Hat is to head as shoe is to _____ .

12. Racquet is to tennis as bat is to _____ .

13. Rome is to Italy as London is to _____ .

14. Boy is to grandpa as girl is to _____ .

15. Mexico is to Mexican as Japan is to _____ .

16. Coyote is to desert as tiger is to _____ .

17. Person is to people as child is to _____ .

18. Caterpillar is to butterfly as tadpole is to _____ .

Dare to Describe

Adjectives and action words help make details come alive.
On the log ride, water went into our log and got us wet.
*On the log ride, **cold** water **splashed** into our log and **soaked** us!*

Rewrite each sentence to make it more descriptive. You can add adjectives, change verbs, or revise the whole sentence.

1. We rode on the roller coaster and went down a hill.

_____

2. We watched floats go by in the parade.

_____

3. The animal show had birds and monkeys.

_____

4. We rode on the bumper cars.

_____

5. My sister didn't want to go on the haunted house ride.

_____

6. We stopped to buy lemonade and take a rest.

_____

7. The Ferris wheel went fast and I got sick.

_____

8. At the arcade, my sister won a prize.

_____

Stem-and-Leaf Graphs

The **stem** is the first digit of a number. The **leaf** is the second digit of a number. Using **stem-and-leaf** graphs is an easy way to find the range, the mode, the median, and the mean of a group of numbers.

Numbers: 56, 33, 45, 49 38, 51, 45

Stems	Leaves
3	3 8
4	5 5 9
5	1 6

Range: 56 – 33 = 23
Mode: 45
Median: 45
Mean: 317 ÷ 7 = 45

Find the range, the mode, the median, and the mean for the numbers in each stem-and-leaf graph. Round to the nearest whole number.

1.

Stems	Leaves
1	3 9
3	5 8 8
4	2 6

Range: _33_
Mode: _38_
Median: _38_
Mean: _33_

2.

Stems	Leaves
7	1 8 9
8	0 4
9	5 7 8 8

Range: _____
Mode: _____
Median: _____
Mean: _____

3.

Stems	Leaves
3	6 6
7	3 4 9
8	2 4 5 7

Range: _____
Mode: _____
Median: _____
Mean: _____

Now, complete each stem-and-leaf graph. Find the range, the mode, the median, and the mean for each group of numbers.

4. 34, 36, 36, 55, 81, 42, 48, 50, 32

Stems	Leaves

Range: _____
Mode: _____
Median: _____
Mean: _____

5. 79, 66, 65, 87, 75, 62, 87, 73, 84

Stems	Leaves

Range: _____
Mode: _____
Median: _____
Mean: _____

Summer Camp

Follow the directions below.

Aaron, Ellie, Jake, and Nicole love summer camp.
Each child has a favorite activity: canoeing, swimming, hiking, and painting.
Which activity is each child's favorite? Use the clues to find your answer.
Hint: Narrow down your choices by crossing them off boxes in the chart.

1. Aaron and Nicole like hiking, but it's not either of their favorite activity.

2. Jake and Ellie's favorite activities are either hiking or swimming.

3. Nicole's best friend thinks painting is the best.

4. Jake's favorite activity used to be swimming.

	Canoeing	Swimming	Hiking	Painting
Aaron				
Ellie				
Jake				
Nicole				

Thank-You Letter

Follow the directions below to write a thank-you letter.

123 Main Street
Littletown, MS 01323
October 17, 2016

Dear Mr. Chase,

    Thank you so much for visiting our class to talk about your work as an astronaut. Your stories were really exciting! The class is now so interested in space travel that we are planning a special field trip to the Air and Space Museum in Washington, D.C. You have really inspired us! We appreciate all the time you spent sharing with us and answering our questions. Please visit again soon!

Sincerely,
Mrs. Dorian's 5th Grade Class

Heading: The heading is your address and the date. Or it can just be the date.

Greeting: This is the opening of the letter. It usually starts with the word *Dear* and ends with a comma.

Body: This is the main part of the letter. Indent each new paragraph.

Closing: This is where the letter ends. It says good-bye with words such as *Sincerely, Your friend, All the best,* or *From.* The first letter in the closing is capitalized and then ends with a comma. It starts halfway across the page.

Signature: This is where you sign your name.

Think of someone who has done something nice for you. On another sheet of paper, write a thank-you letter to him or her. Explain to this person how much you appreciate what he or she did for you.

Remember to follow these rules:
- Use interesting, specific words.
- Use correct punctuation.
- Use complete sentences.

Barbecue Bests

Follow the directions below.

Circle the best unit for measuring each object.

1. The length of a   (inches)   feet   miles

2. The height of a   inches   feet   miles

3. The distance to the   inches   feet   miles

4. The length of an   centimeters   meters   kilometers

Circle the best weight estimate for each object.

5.   12 ounces   12 pounds   12 tons

6.   200 ounces   200 pounds   200 tons

7.   3 ounces   3 pounds   3 tons

8.   2 ounces   2 pounds   2 tons

Max's Market

Read the prices for items sold at Max's Market.
Use the information to solve the problems.

Max's Market

Peas 13¢ per oz.   Lettuce $1.15 per head
Corn 50¢ per cob   Red Onions $1.20 per lb.
Celery 10¢ per oz.   Sweet Onions $1.45 per lb.
Carrots 12¢ per oz.   Spinach 75¢ per bunch
Tomatoes 15¢ per oz.   Garlic 45¢ per bulb

*16 ounces (oz.) = 1 pound (lb.)

1. Jamie bought $\frac{1}{2}$ pound of peas, 2 pounds of carrots, 4 cobs of corn, and 1 pound of tomatoes. How much did he spend? ___$9.28___

2. Celery and carrots are on sale for half off today! Ming bought 5 pounds of carrots and 5 pounds of celery. How much did he spend? _____

3. Kylie loaded up on onions, tomatoes, and garlic for her special spaghetti sauce. She needs 4 pounds of tomatoes, 6 bulbs of garlic, and 2 pounds of sweet onions. How much did she spend? _____
She paid with a $20 bill. How much change did she receive? _____

4. All green vegetables are on special today. Buy one pound and get the second pound free! Or, buy one item and get the second item free! Tyler stocked up on 4 pounds of each green vegetable. He also bought 4 heads of lettuce and 4 bunches of spinach. How much did he spend?

_____

5. Carla bought 2 heads of lettuce, 4 bulbs of garlic, 3 bunches of spinach, and 6 cobs of corn. How much did she spend?

_____

6. Brian needs 1 pound of each vegetable sold per pound or per ounce at Max's Market. How much did he spend?
_____ He paid with three $5 bills. How much change did he receive?

_____

7. For the holiday, Max reduced the price of each item 5¢. Hanna bought 3 pounds each of red and sweet onions, 3 heads of lettuce, and 3 bunches of spinach. How much did she spend? _____

8. Corey accidentally knocked over the basket of tomatoes, and 4 of the 15 pounds were ruined! Corey felt bad and decided to buy the rest of the good tomatoes. How much did he spend? _____

Abstract Nouns

Concrete nouns are things you can see, hear, smell, taste, or feel. **Abstract** nouns, on the other hand, are ideas such as knowledge, happiness, and brotherhood.

Use the graph to find the abstract nouns below. Each column has a number and each row has a letter. Use the letter and number coordinates to solve the noun puzzles.

Example: 6B = E

	1	2	3	4	5	6	7	8
A	A	K	L	O	R	B	U	X
B	G	D	P	I	V	E	S	N
C	H	T	C	Y	A	W	J	M
D	O	G	E	D	P	H	U	R
E	Y	I	S	W	F	N	K	L
F	E	T	D	M	H	O	Z	C
G	J	A	Q	P	R	I	H	B
H	V	N	F	E	W	S	K	U

1. _f_ _r_ _i_ _e_ _n_ _d_ _s_ _h_ _i_ _p_
   5E 8D 2E 4H 6E 2B 7B 1C 6G 5D

2. ___ ___ ___ ___ ___ ___
   4E 2E 7B 3F 4A 8C

3. ___ ___ ___ ___
   3A 6F 1H 6B

4. ___ ___ ___ ___ ___ ___ ___ ___ ___ ___ ___ ___ ___
   7D 2H 4D 3D 5G 3E 2F 1A 8B 2B 2E 6E 1B

5. ___ ___ ___ ___ ___ ___
   5H 3D 2G 8E 2F 7G

6. ___ ___ ___ ___ ___ ___ ___
   3H 8D 6B 4H 3F 4A 4F

7. ___ ___ ___
   7C 6F 4C

8. ___ ___ ___ ___ ___ ___ ___ ___ ___ ___ ___ ___
   2E 8B 2C 6B 8E 3A 2E 1B 3D 2H 8F 1F

Which of these abstract nouns would you like to have the most? Why?

_____

_____

Search for the Source

Seventy-five percent of Earth's surface is covered in water. More than 97 percent of this water is in the ocean. Only about 3 percent of Earth's surface is freshwater, or water that is not in the ocean.

Water Source	Percentage of Total Water*
Oceans	97.24%
Ice Caps, Glaciers	2.14%
Groundwater	.61%
Freshwater Lakes	.009%
Inland Seas	.008%
Soil Moisture	.005%
Atmosphere	.001%
Rivers	.001%

Find each of the water sources in the word search below.

```
F  R  E  S  H  W  A  T  E  R  L  A  K  E  S
R  I  L  S  H  S  O  I  O  M  O  T  F  R  O
O  V  A  R  I  V  L  K  C  R  S  M  O  C  I
C  E  K  G  O  C  A  R  E  F  G  O  N  D  L
A  I  N  L  A  N  D  S  E  A  S  S  G  H  M
N  C  I  A  S  O  L  I  N  L  A  P  N  D  O
W  E  L  C  G  R  O  U  S  O  L  H  M  O  I
T  C  A  I  W  A  T  R  I  V  G  E  G  L  S
R  A  N  E  I  C  A  P  S  G  L  R  K  E  T
A  P  S  R  I  V  E  R  S  R  L  E  K  E  U
T  S  E  S  G  R  O  U  N  D  W  A  T  E  R
M  G  A  S  I  N  L  O  C  E  A  N  S  V  E
```

*Percentages are rounded, so will not add up to 100.

A Whale Tale

Read the passage. Then complete the graphic organizer.

There are more than 75 different types of whales swimming in our ocean. Some weigh in at 150 tons, and others are just a few feet long. But all whales, no matter how big or small, can be classified into two groups: toothed whales and baleen whales.

Toothed whales have sharp teeth for eating fish and plants. Dolphins and porpoises are actually types of toothed whales. The killer whale is another type of toothed whale.

Baleen whales do not have any teeth. They have plates attached to their jawbones. Baleen whales simply open their mouths and suck in seawater. The plates filter out plankton and krill for the whale to eat. Baleen whales are sometimes called filter feeders. Some types of baleen whales include blue whales, humpback whales, and gray whales.

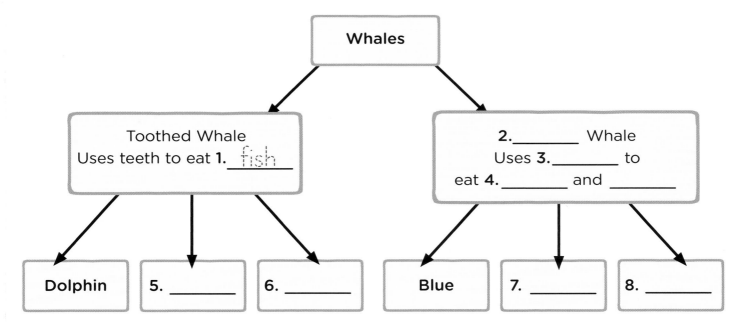

Whales

Toothed Whale
Uses teeth to eat **1.** _fish_

2._____ Whale
Uses **3.**_____ to
eat **4.**_____ and _____

Dolphin

5. _____

6. _____

Blue

7. _____

8. _____

Do You Measure Up?

Use the measurements in the box to solve the problems.
Round to the nearest whole number if needed.

12 inches = 1 foot	3 feet = 1 yard
1,760 yards = 1 mile	1 foot = .30 meter
1 meter = 3.28 feet	100 centimeters = 1 meter
1,000 meters = 1 kilometer	1.6 kilometers = 1 mile
1 kilometer = .62 mile	

1. Brandon runs four 10-mile marathons per year.

How many kilometers does he run per year? _____64 kilometers_____

How many yards does he run per year? _____70,400 yards_____

2. Jun needs 8 yards of ribbon to trim the dresses.

How many feet does she need? _____

How many inches does she need? _____

3. The school pool is 20 meters long and 40 meters wide.

How many meters is the perimeter? _____

How many centimeters is the perimeter? _____

4. Justin is 6 feet, 2 inches tall.

How many inches tall is he? _____

About how many meters tall is he? _____

5. Keisha drives 18 kilometers to work each day.

How many meters does she drive round trip? _____

How many miles does she drive round trip? _____

6. Shane measured his bedroom to lay new carpet. His room is 15 feet by 18 feet.

How many meters is the perimeter of his bedroom? _____

How many yards is the perimeter of his bedroom? _____

Improve Your Sentences

Good writing contains specific details and descriptions. To make sentences even better, ask yourself these questions: **Who? What? Where? When? Why? How?**

Example:
The horse ran.

What kind? | **Where?** | **When?**
Beautiful chestnut | Across the beach | At sunset

New Sentence: The beautiful chestnut horse ran across the beach at sunset.

Now try your hand at making these sentences better. Remember to think *who, what, where, when, why,* and *how.*

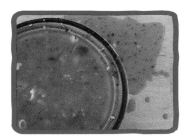

1. The soup spilled. _____

2. The giant roared. _____

3. Jen loves flowers. _____

4. The race car crashed. _____

5. Dogs do tricks. _____

6. Mom baked bread. _____

7. Tanner likes to paint. _____

8. The wind blew. _____

9. I like cookies. _____

10. Nate laughed. _____

Camp Clearlake

A word that ends in **ing** can be part of a **verb** or it can be a **noun**. A noun that ends in **ing** is called a **gerund**.

Verbs: I went skating.
Let's go walking.
Gerunds: Skating on the ice is fun.
I like walking in the woods.

Figure out if the underlined word in each sentence is a verb or a gerund, then circle the correct term for each.

1. Most campers went <u>hiking</u> in the hills every day.   Verb   Gerund

2. <u>Fishing</u> was a fun way to spend the afternoon.   Verb   Gerund

3. Campers said that <u>swimming</u> was their favorite activity.   Verb   Gerund

4. The older campers went <u>biking</u> on mountain trails.   Verb   Gerund

5. <u>Boating</u> on the lake was not allowed when it was raining.   Verb   Gerund

6. Every night the campers were <u>singing</u> around the campfire.   Verb   Gerund

7. All the campers helped with the <u>cleaning</u> after dinner.   Verb   Gerund

8. Campers could take lessons to improve their horseback <u>riding</u>.   Verb   Gerund

Types of Triangles

Follow the directions below.

Look at the types of triangles.
Then label each triangle below.

An **equilateral triangle** has all congruent sides.

An **isosceles triangle** has two congruent sides.

A **scalene triangle** has no congruent sides.

A **right triangle** has one right angle.

The angles of a triangle always add up to 180.

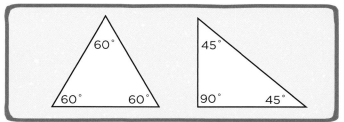

Figure out if the number of degrees in the third angle of each triangle.

6.

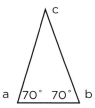

c = ___40___

7.

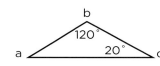

a = _____

8.

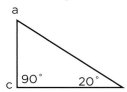

c = _____

9.

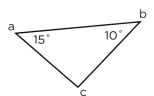

a = _____

10.

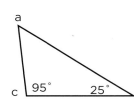

a = _____

1.

equilateral

2.

_____

3.

_____

4.

_____

5.

_____

Football Fever

Use the clues to find the answers. Write your answers in the puzzle.

Touchdown = 6 points
Field goal = 3 points
Safety = 2 points
Extra point = 1 point*

Game = 4 quarters
Football field = 100 yards
First down = 10 yards
Personal foul = 15 yards

*Whenever a team scores a touchdown, it gets a chance to kick an extra point.

Solve these problems about football using the information above.

1. The Cheetahs scored 3 touchdowns in the first quarter and 2 in the fourth quarter. They missed two extra points. The Mustangs scored 2 touchdowns in the second quarter, 1 in the third quarter, and 3 field goals in the fourth quarter. They made all their extra points. Who won the game? The Cheetahs
What was the final score? Cheetahs _____
Mustangs _____

2. Cheetah Jackson Biggs ran from his own 20 yard line to the other team's 42 yard line. How many yards did he gain?_____
How many more yards would he have to gain to get to the Mustangs' end zone and score a touchdown? _____

3. Mustang quarterback Manny Garcia threw the ball from his own 25 yard line. It was caught 50 yards down the field. On what yard line was the ball caught? _____
What percentage of the field did the Mustangs cover? _____

4. The Mustangs gained 86 yards in the first quarter and 110 yards in the second quarter. They also got called for three personal fouls.
How many total yards did they gain by halftime?_____

5. The Cheetahs are on their own 30 yard line. How many yards do they need to reach the Mustangs' end zone to score a touchdown?_____
How many first downs do they need? _____

6. Mustang Alex Shaw kicked a field goal to win the game by 1 point! The Cheetahs had scored 5 touchdowns, 3 extra points, and 2 field goals. What was the final score?
Cheetahs _____   Mustangs _____

Good Connections

Conjunctions such as **and** and **or** can connect two or more simple subjects to form a compound subject. Compound subjects share the same predicate.

Example:
Kittens are soft. Puppies are soft.
Kittens and puppies are soft

Use **and** or **or** to write a sentence with a compound subject.

1. Josh is a student in Mr. Chang's class. Maria is a student in Mr. Chang's class. _____Josh and Maria are students in Mr. Chang's Class._____

2. Jaguars live in the rain forest. Toucans live in the rain forest.
_____

3. Tina is a talented dancer. Shiki is a talented dancer. Sonya is a talented dancer.
_____

4. Blue whales are mammals that live in the ocean. Dolphins are mammals that live in the ocean. _____

5. Shells are on the beach. Starfish are on the beach. Crabs are on the beach.
_____

Conjunctions such as **and**, **but**, and **or** can connect two or more simple predicates to form a compound predicate. Compound predicates share the same subject.

Example:
The pizza is cold. The pizza is delicious.
The pizza is cold but delicious.

Use **and**, **or**, or **but** to write a sentence with a compound predicate.

6. Cats are fun. Cats are lovable. Cats can be difficult to train.
_____

7. Cell phones are good for safety. Cell phones can be annoying to people around you.
_____

8. Red fire ants should be left alone. Red fire ants should be removed by a professional.
_____

9. Daniel runs very fast. Daniel doesn't like football.
_____

10. Trina lives in the mountains. Trina grows all of her food.
_____

Quadrilateral Quiz

A **quadrilateral** is a four-sided shape. The angles in a quadrilateral always add up to 360 degrees.

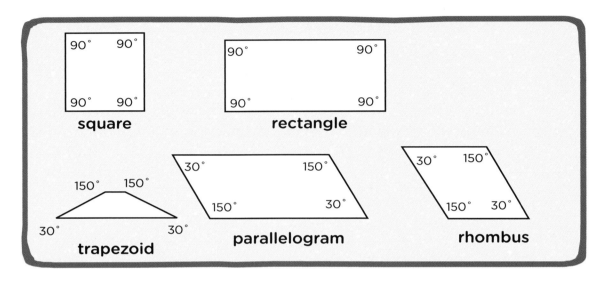

square

rectangle

trapezoid

parallelogram

rhombus

Label each shape and figure out the number of degrees in the fourth angle. Remember, the angles will all add up to 360.

1.

A 90° 90° B

D 90° C

square

D = _90°_

2. A 45° 135° B

C 45° D

_____

C = _____

3.

D C 155°
25° 25°
A B

_____

D = _____

4.

A 15°
165° B
D 15°
C

_____

D = _____

5.

A 120° B
60° 120°
D C

_____

B = _____

6.

A 140° B
140° 40°
D C

_____

A = _____

7.

A B
90°
D 90° 90° C

_____

A = _____

8.

A 90° B
90° 90°
D C

_____

B = _____

Portrait of a Hero

Read the passage and answer the questions below.

On a hot summer day in 1778, General Washington's army battled against the British near Monmouth, New Jersey. In the midst of flying bullets, a woman named Mary Ludwig Hays McCauly was busy helping the soldiers. The men called her Molly Pitcher because she brought pitchers of cool water to tired, thirsty soldiers on the field.

Molly's husband, William Hays, was one of the soldiers in the battle. When he fell wounded, Molly quickly took his place and manned the cannon. Even during heavy enemy fire, Molly stayed behind the cannon and fired back. She also helped take care of the wounded soldiers. One time, she carried a wounded soldier off the battlefield to safety.

For her heroic actions, General Washington made her a noncommissioned officer. After this, she was known as Sergeant Molly. If you visit the battle site, you'll see a sculpture of Sergeant Molly on the battle monument.

Write some words that describe the qualities of a hero.

_____ brave _____   _____

_____   _____

_____   _____

_____

What actions show that Molly Pitcher was a hero?

_____

_____

_____

_____

_____

_____

Surf's Up!

Read the following passage. Then answer the questions.

Surfers seem to have a language all their own. Some people might think that "surf bum" and "dude" are the only real surf terms, but think again! Surfing has its own special lingo. For example, a "slash" is a rapid turn off a wave that creates a big spray. A "tube" is when the wave is hollow where it is breaking. For some surfers, a tube is the peak experience of surfing. A "stick" is a surfboard, and a "swell" is a group of waves. A "rip" is a strong current running out to sea, and a "goofy foot" is surfing with your right foot forward. There are other things you should be aware of as you're riding the waves. In the surfing world, you never want to "drop in." This is when a surfer catches a wave when he or she does not have priority. In other  words, there is another surfer already on the wave. You also never want to "wipe out," or fall off your board. Other terms for wiping out are "mullering," "donut," "eating it," and "pounding." So, just do your best to "hang ten" on the "gnarly" waves! You'll be "stoked"!

1. What do some consider the peak experience of surfing?

_____

_____

2. Based on the surrounding text, what do you think the word *lingo* means?

_____

_____

3. What should you never do when surfing?

_____

_____

4. What are three other terms for "wiping out"?

_____

_____

5. What is the term for surfing with your right foot forward?

_____

6. Based on the surrounding text, what do you think the word *stoked* means?

_____

Sue's Clues

A **conclusion** is when you use clues to find out something that is not directly stated.

Read each set of clues and circle the best conclusion.

1.

Sue visited a friend who had the flu.

That night, Sue started sneezing.

The next day, Sue had a fever.

a) Sue was upset with her friend.
b) Sue caught the flu from her friend.
c) Sue's friend is feeling better.

2.

Sue came home to a messy bedroom.

Some of her shoes were chewed up.

Sue saw muddy paw prints on the carpet.

a) Sue's little brother messed up her room.
b) Sue always has a messy room.
c) Sue's dog messed up her room.

Read the story. Look for the clues that led to Sue's conclusion and write them on the lines below.

Whenever Sue made cookies, she always brought some to her next-door-neighbor Mrs. Taylor. One night, Sue took some cookies over to Mrs. Taylor's house and rang the doorbell. Nobody was home. The house was very dark.

Sue decided that she would leave the cookies in Mrs. Taylor's mailbox. But there was no room because the mailbox was full of mail! Nobody had gotten the mail for a few days. Sue also noticed that a few newspapers were stacked on Mrs. Taylor's porch.

For the next few days, Sue watched Mrs. Taylor's house. She didn't see Mrs. Taylor come home. She concluded that Mrs. Taylor must be on vacation. So, Sue ate all the cookies by herself!

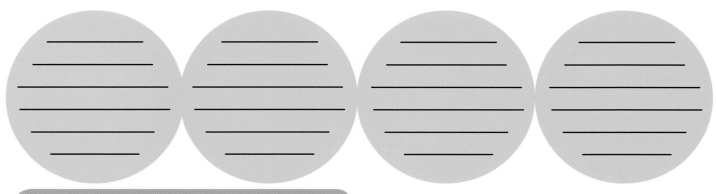

Conclusion: Mrs. Taylor is on vacation.

Fraction Add-venture

To add two like fractions, add only the numerators.

$$\frac{2}{6} + \frac{1}{6} = \frac{3}{6} = \frac{1}{2}$$

$$\frac{2}{4} + \frac{3}{4} = \frac{5}{4} = 1\frac{1}{4}$$

Add the fractions. Show the answers in lowest terms.

1. $\frac{2}{10} + \frac{4}{10} = \frac{6}{10} = \frac{3}{5}$

2. $\frac{5}{8} + \frac{1}{8} = \underline{} = \underline{}$

3. $\frac{1}{2} + \frac{1}{2} = \underline{} = \underline{}$

4. $\frac{3}{5} + \frac{3}{5} = \underline{} = \underline{}$

5. $\frac{2}{7} + \frac{3}{7} = \underline{} = \underline{}$

6. $\frac{4}{8} + \frac{1}{8} = \underline{} = \underline{}$

7. $\frac{1}{12} + \frac{5}{12} = \underline{} = \underline{}$

8. $\frac{6}{11} + \frac{4}{11} = \underline{} = \underline{}$

9. $\frac{3}{6} + \frac{1}{6} = \underline{} = \underline{}$

10. $\frac{2}{3} + \frac{2}{3} = \underline{} = \underline{}$

Dare with Decimals

Answer the questions below.

Which number in each group has the largest value? Circle your answer.

1. 0.075
   7.50
   .0075
   (75.00)

2. 5.550
   05.50
   55.05
   5.055

3. 0.024
   0.0204
   .0024
   2.04

4. 9.035
   0.935
   .0935
   0.0095

Which number in each group has the smallest value? Circle your answer.

5. 0.3
   0.03
   0.003
   0.0003

6. 0.850
   8.005
   8.050
   0.0085

7. 1.270
   .0127
   12.170
   1.207

8. 0.006
   0.060
   0.0006
   6.00

Write these numbers in order from least to greatest.

9. 0.058, 0.0058, 5.80, 0.580, 58.0

_____ , _____ , _____ , _____ , _____

10. 0.10, 10.01, 1.001, 100.10, 0.001

_____ , _____ , _____ , _____ , _____

11. 9.910, .0910, 0.0091, 9,001, 9.010

_____ , _____ , _____ , _____ , _____

12. 537.00, 0.00537, 5.371, 53.07, 0.0537

_____ , _____ , _____ , _____ , _____

Writing Styles

Follow the directions below.

There are many different styles of writing. Here are a few.
Expository writing gives information and facts. **Narrative** writing tells a story.
Descriptive writing "paints a picture" of a person, a place, or a thing.
Persuasive writing tries to convince someone of something.

Read each prompt below. Then write the style of writing needed—**expository**,
narrative, **descriptive**, or **persuasive**.

1. _narrative_ You went camping on the beach with your
family. Tell about your experiences exploring the tide pools
and watching the sun set over the ocean. Tell about any
special adventures you had.

2. _____ Give instructions on how to fix a flat tire.
Write the steps in order so people can follow them easily.

3. _____ Write an article convincing people why it's important to save the rain
forests. Support your argument with facts about the negative effects of thousands of
acres being destroyed every day.

4. _____ Imagine you are sitting in the middle of a spring meadow. You hear the
bees buzzing; you see the grass waving in the breeze. Write details about all the other
things you see, hear, smell, taste, and feel.

5. _____ Write an informative article about the pack behavior of wolves in the
wild. Explain how packs live and stay together.

6. _____ Do you remember an exciting or memorable birthday? Write about the
special events of that day and the gifts you received.

7. _____ Write a letter to your parents giving reasons why you should have a later
bedtime. Convince your parents why this would benefit them as well as you.

8. _____ Think about your favorite food. Describe it in detail. Is it spicy or hot?
Is it sweet or sugary? Describe how it smells, tastes, and feels in your mouth.

How Low Can You Go?

Unlike fractions do not have the same denominator. To add or subtract unlike fractions, you have to find the **least common denominator**, or the **LCD**.

$\frac{1}{6}$ and $\frac{1}{4}$ are unlike fractions.

The lowest number that can be divided by both 6 and 4 is 12.

$\frac{1}{6} = \frac{2}{12}$

$\frac{1}{4} = \frac{3}{12}$

The lowest common denominator of **6** and **4** is **12**.

Use the LCD to convert the unlike fractions to like fractions.

1. $\frac{1}{3}$, $\frac{1}{2}$ $\frac{2}{6}$, $\frac{3}{6}$

LCD 6

2. $\frac{2}{3}$, $\frac{1}{6}$ ___ , ___

LCD 6

3. $\frac{3}{5}$, $\frac{1}{3}$ ___ , ___

LCD 15

4. $\frac{4}{8}$, $\frac{3}{4}$ ___ , ___

LCD 8

Find the LCD for each pair of fractions.

5. $\frac{2}{4}$, $\frac{1}{3}$

LCD = ___

6. $\frac{5}{6}$, $\frac{4}{9}$

LCD = ___

7. $\frac{3}{10}$, $\frac{1}{4}$

LCD = ___

8. $\frac{2}{3}$, $\frac{8}{9}$

LCD = ___

Lines, Shapes, and Angles

Look at each group of figures. Then answer the question by circling the correct answer.

1. Which figure has a right angle?

a) 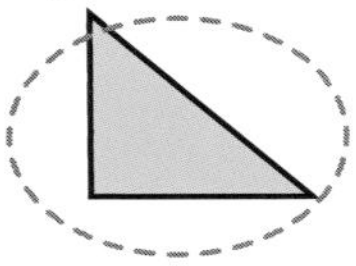   b)    c)

2. Which figure has 6 surfaces?

a)    b) 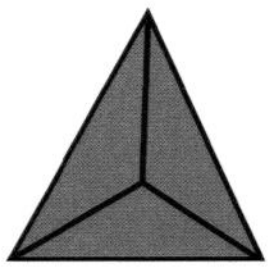   c)

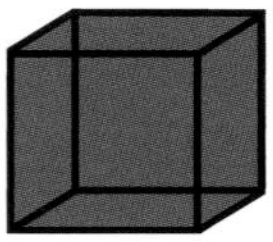

3. Which pair of lines is perpendicular?

a) 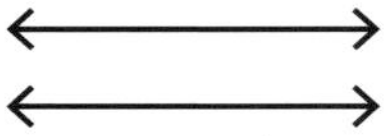   b) 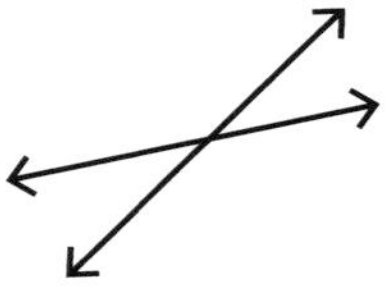   c)

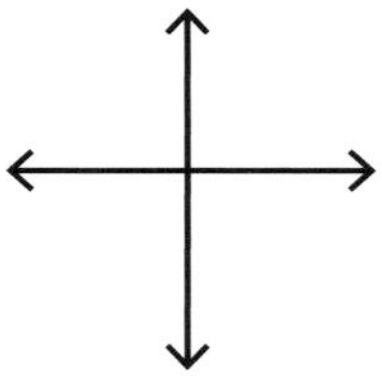

4. Which figure shows an obtuse angle?

a) 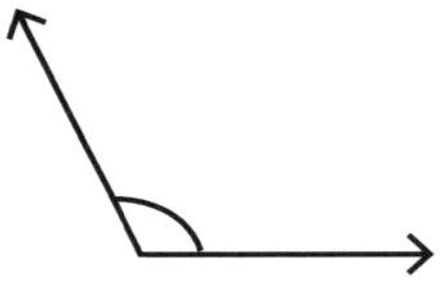   b) 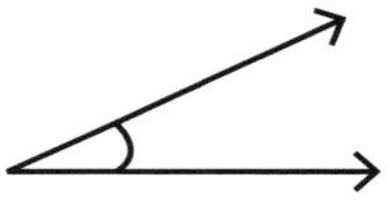   c)

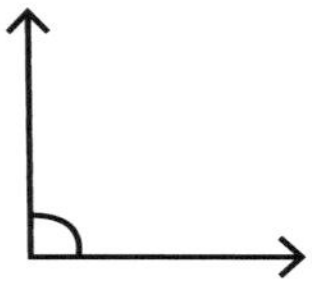

5. Which figure is an equilateral triangle?

a) 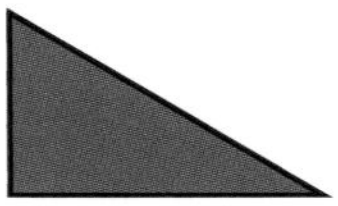   b) 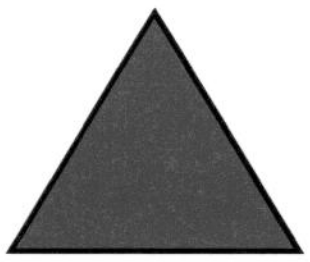   c)

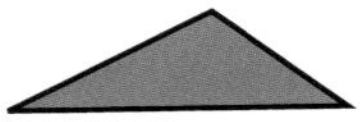

6. Which line shows the radius?

a) 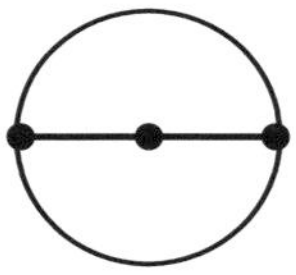   b)    c)

7. Which figure shows an acute angle?

a) 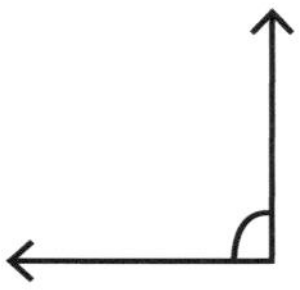   b) 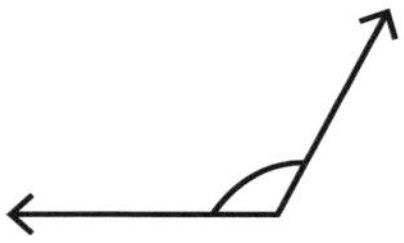   c)

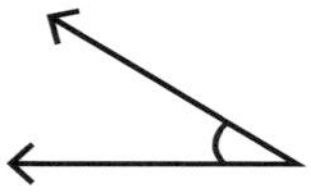

8. Which pair of lines is parallel?

a) 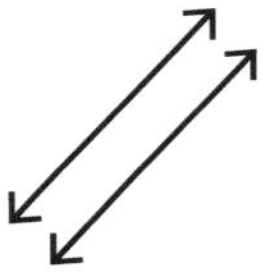   b) 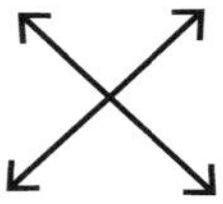   c)

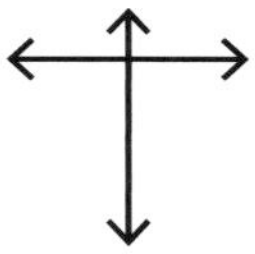

Writing to Persuade

Persuasive writing tries to convince someone of something. The writer gives the pros or the cons of the subject and tries to get readers to agree with his or her point of view. The writer must use reasons to support his or her opinion.

Choose one of these topics to write about:
- Should students be required to wear school uniforms?
- Should you be able to have any kind of pet you choose?
- Should you be able to watch television whenever you want?
- Should the school allow you to choose the subjects you want to study?

Use this graphic organizer to write your ideas. You can write words, phrases, or sentences.

Topic: _____

First Paragraph

In my opinion

Three reasons that support my opinion, and examples to support each one:

Paragraph 2

Reason 1	Examples or details

Paragraph 3

Reason 2	Examples or details

Last Paragraph

In my opinion

Use your ideas from the graphic organizer to write a persuasive essay on a separate sheet of paper.

A Super Star

Read the passage and answer the questions below.

What gives us heat, light, warmth, and energy and is at the center of our solar system? The sun! The sun is actually a star, just like the other stars you see in the night sky. The sun, like all stars, is made of gas. At the center, or core, of the sun, hydrogen gas is turned into helium gas. This reaction gives off heat and light.

The sun is very hot. On the surface it's about 10,832 degrees Farenheit (6,000 degrees Celsius.) The atmosphere around the surface is even hotter, with temperatures in the millions of degrees. Some spots on the sun's surface appear darker because they are slightly cooler. These are called sunspots.

Most people think that stars are smaller than planets, but the sun is much bigger than Earth. About 109 planets the size of Earth would fit across the diameter of the sun. If the sun were hollow, about a million Earths would fit inside. Practically everything on Earth depends on the sun, including people, plants, and animals. It really is a super star!

1. What happens in the sun's core? _Hydrogen gas is turned into helium gas._

2. How hot is the sun? _____

_____

3. What are sunspots? _____

_____

4. How big is the sun compared to Earth? _____

_____

5. Why is the sun important to us here on Earth? _____

_____

A Reason for the Season

Persuasive writing gives an argument and supports it with reasons. Read each passage. Then summarize the author's argument and the reasons given to support it.

Summer Is Super

Summer is the best season of the year. First of all, warm summer weather is great. The sun shines almost every day, so you can be outdoors all the time, even at night! Because of the warm weather, summer is perfect for swimming, hiking, or boating.

Of course, the best thing about summer is that you have a vacation from school. You can relax, travel, and spend time with your friends and family. Summer offers more freedom and fun than any other season!

1. Argument: The best season of the year is _____.
2. Reasons: _____

_____

_____

Wonderful Winter

Winter is the best season because it has something to offer everyone. If you like to stay indoors, winter is perfect for curling up beside a fire. If you like to be outdoors, you can ski, snowboard, or sled in the winter snow. Bundling up in coats and scarves is always fun.

Winter is very special because there are so many festive holidays to celebrate. Family and friends come together to share these special times. Winter is the perfect time to make special memories.

3. Argument: The best season of the year is _____.
4. Reasons: _____

_____

5. Which argument to do you agree with and why? _____

_____

_____

_____

Calling All Cooks!

Follow the directions below.

Wendy is making chocolate cake for the party. When more people decided to come, she made 5 more cakes. Then even more people decided to come! She made 8 more cakes. Write how much of each ingredient she needed. Hint: Read the measurement equivalents in the box to find your answers.

3 tsp. = 1 Tbsp.   8 oz. = 1 cup   2 cups = 1 pint   2 pints = 1 quart   4 quarts = 1 gallon

Double Chocolate Tower Cake

1 Cake	5 Cakes	8 Cakes
1 cup butter, softened	5 cups	8 cups
1 Tbsp. instant coffee		
$1\frac{1}{3}$ cups water		
8 oz. chocolate chips		
5 eggs		
2 tsp. vanilla		
$2\frac{1}{4}$ cups flour		
$1\frac{1}{2}$ Tbsp. baking powder		
$\frac{1}{2}$ tsp. salt		
$1\frac{1}{2}$ tsp. cinnamon		

Chocolate Fudge Icing

1 Batch	5 Batches	8 Batches
$\frac{3}{4}$ cup heavy cream		
6 oz. chocolate chips		
$\frac{1}{4}$ tsp. vanilla		
3 cups powdered sugar		
2 Tbsp. milk		

Writing Titles

Follow the directions below.

Rewrite each title using correct capitalization and punctuation.

> **Underline** or **italicize** the titles of books, plays, paintings, magazines, newspapers, television shows, CDs, and movies.
>
> Put **quotation marks** around titles of poems, short stories, book chapters, magazine and newspaper articles, and songs.
>
> **Do Not Capitalize:**
> - Short prepositions (**at, by, in, of, for, with, to**)
> - Short conjunctions (**and, but, or**)
> - Articles (**a, an, the**) unless they are the final word in a title

1. tales of a fourth grade nothing (book)

Tales of a Fourth Grade Nothing

2. mona lisa (painting)

_____

3. if i had a brontosaurus (poem)

_____

4. harry potter and the chamber of secrets (movie)

_____

5. legends of the hidden temple (TV show)

_____

6. america the beautiful (song)

_____

7. if i were in charge of the world and other worries (book)

_____

8. los angeles times (newspaper)

_____

9. sports illustrated for kids (magazine)

_____

10. lost in the middle of the night (chapter title)

_____

11. romeo and juliet (play)

_____

12. how the tiger got its stripes (short story)

_____

Write a sentence using each title. Remember to capitalize and punctuate it correctly.

13. ten tricks to teach your dog (magazine article)

_____

14. farmer in the dell (song)

_____

15. julie of the wolves (book)

_____

16. the road to rock and roll (CD)

_____

Hooray for Holidays!

Come up with a new holiday that you think
should be added to the calendar.

First, brainstorm some ideas about your holiday. What makes this holiday special?
How would people celebrate it? Why should it be added to the calendar?

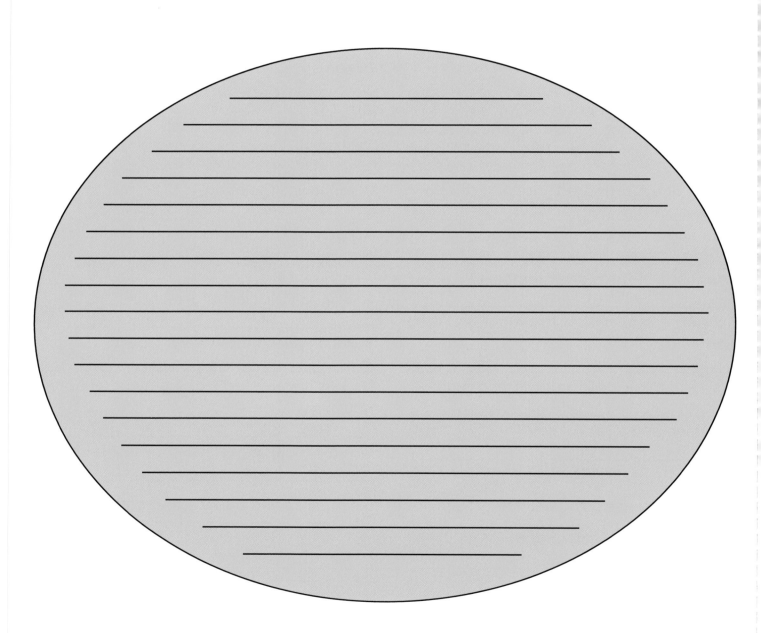

On a separate piece of paper use your ideas to write a persuasive paragraph. Try to
convince someone that your holiday should be celebrated. Include lots of reasons to
support your point!

Shape Up

Follow the directions below.

The **perimeter** of a shape is the sum of all the sides added together.
The **area of a quadrilateral** = length × height.
The **area of a triangle** = $\frac{1}{2}$ × length × height.

Perimeter = 50 + 50 + 20 + 20 = 140 yards
Area = 50 × 20 = 1,000 yards²

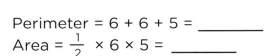

50 yards

20 yards   20 yards

50 yards

Perimeter = 6 + 3 + 7 = 16 feet
Area = $\frac{1}{2}$ × 3 × 6 = 9 feet²

6 feet   7 feet

3 feet

1.

7 inches

4 inches

2.

6 cm.

5 cm

6 cm.

Perimeter = 7 + 7 + 4 + 4 = _____
Area = 7 × 4 = _____

Perimeter = 6 + 6 + 5 = _____
Area = $\frac{1}{2}$ × 6 × 5 = _____

3.

3 yards

3 yards   3 yards

3 yards

4.

12 ft.   15 ft.

9 ft.

Perimeter: _____
Area: _____

Perimeter: _____
Area: _____

5.

10 inches

4 inches

6.

7 ft.

2 ft.

Perimeter: _____
Area: _____

Perimeter: _____
Area: _____

Dog Walkers

Read the paragraph. Then fill in the chart.

Kevin, Luke, Mira, Tia, and Raul all work as dog walkers to make extra money. Each has a favorite kind of dog. The dogs are dalmatians, poodles, beagles, labs, and huskies. What is each child's favorite dog? Use the clues to find your answer.
Hint: Narrow down your choices by crossing off boxes in the chart.

1. Tham likes beagles less than her favorite, huskies.
2. Raul and Luke do not like labs or beagles.
3. Kevin and the child who likes labs are best friends.
4. Either Luke or Mira likes poodles the best.

Fill in the names of the children down the side of the chart.
Write the names of the dogs across the top of the chart.
Now, solve the problem!

Great Words: Thesaurus

Use a thesaurus to find another word to replace the underlined words in the sentences below. Rewrite the sentence using a new word.

A **thesaurus** is a reference that contains synonyms and antonyms for words. As in a dictionary, words are listed in alphabetical order. Many words have slight differences in meaning. By choosing words carefully, a writer can create a clear picture for the reader.

1. "Watch out! That snake could bite you!" <u>said</u> Viet.

_____

2. Jason slipped and <u>fell</u> down the slippery steps.

_____

3. The hikers were <u>hungry</u> when they returned to camp.

_____

4. The mouse <u>ran</u> back to its hole when it saw the cat.

_____

5. Party guests complimented the chef on the <u>good</u> meal.

_____

6. I was too <u>nervous</u> to go to bed after watching the scary movie.

_____

7. Our football team was <u>excited</u> after winning the game.

_____

8. The mountain looked <u>huge</u> against the clear blue sky.

_____

9. <u>Angry</u> fans yelled in protest over the umpire's bad call.

_____

10. I made sure the house was as <u>clean</u> as possible for my guests.

_____

Book Report

It's time to write your very own book report! First, choose a book that tells a story. After you read it, complete the sentences below.

Book Title: _____

Author: _____

This story is about _____ .

The main characters are _____ .

_____ is _____ .
(character name)   (describe the character)

_____ is _____ .
(a different character name)   (describe the character)

The story takes place in _____ .

The mood of the story is _____ .

The main conflict in the story is _____

_____ .

The resolution happens when _____

_____ .

The theme of the story is _____

_____ .

I would / would not recommend this book to a friend because _____

_____

_____ .

Bar Graphs

Read the information in the bar graph. Then answer the questions.

Favorite Sports Survey

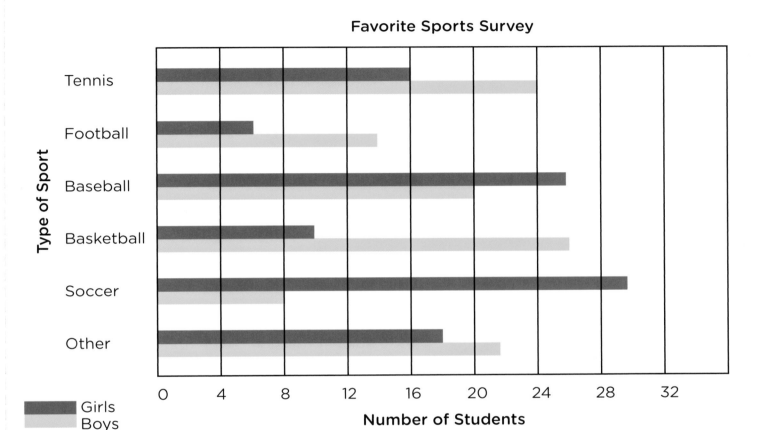

Type of Sport / Number of Students

Legend:
- Girls
- Boys

1. How many girls like baseball best? _____26_____
2. How many boys like tennis best? _____
3. How many boys and girls like soccer? _____
4. How many more boys like basketball than girls? _____
5. Which sport do boys like best? _____ Girls? _____
6. How many total students were surveyed? _____

Using Figurative Language

Read the paragraph below. Then answer the questions.

Some terms sound like what they mean.
> **crackling fire**   **gurgling creek**

Some terms describe things by comparing them to something else.
> **shy as a mouse**   **tall as a mountain**

Some terms make things "come alive" by giving them human qualities.
> **dancing rain**   **whispering breeze**

Terms can also be used to create vivid, detailed descriptions.
Okay: Small spiders went up the drainpipe.
Better: Tiny spiders scrambled up the drainpipe.

I woke up suddenly in the middle of the night. Darkness filled my room like a thick blanket. I heard the wind moaning outside my window. The trees bent in the wind, holding onto their leaves like protective mothers. As I peeked out my window, not even a friendly moon greeted me. Not one star peeked out from behind the velvet veil of the black sky. Branches screeched and clattered against the side of the house. I hoped morning would soon show her cheery face.

1. Write two comparisons used in the paragraph.

_____

_____

2. What human qualities does the writer give the moon? _____

3. What human qualities does the writer give the morning? _____

4. What terms are used to describe the night sky? _____

5. Which two words sound like what they mean? What are they describing?

_____

_____

Write a creative sentence about each of the following topics. Use one example of figurative language described above.

6. pouring rain _____

7. purring kitten _____

8. haunted house _____

State Report

Look up your state in an encyclopedia. Fill in the blanks below with information about the state you live in. When you're done, you'll have a State Report!

State Name: _____

Population: _____

Capital City: _____

Largest City: _____

State Motto: _____

_____

State Bird: _____

State Flower: _____

Natural Features:

What kind of physical features does your state have? Are there mountain ranges, rivers, deserts, or lakes? Name some of these features and describe them.

_____
_____
_____
_____
_____

Climate:

What kind of weather does your state have? How much rainfall and snowfall does the state get in a year? What is the average temperature?

_____
_____
_____
_____
_____

History:

How and when did your state become a state? Name a historic person or place in your state.

_____
_____
_____
_____
_____
_____
_____
_____

Follow the Clues

Follow the clues to solve the problems.

Clues

1. Each problem has two steps.

2. Use **( )** as your first step to close off two numbers.

3. Use two operation signs (**×, −, +, ÷**).

4. Use one equals sign (**=**).

Example: 16 _____ 4 _____ 8 _____ 32

Answer: (16 ÷ 4) × 8 = 32

1. 28 _____ 7 _____ 8 _____ 28

2. 77 _____ 13 _____ 3 _____ 38

3. 80 _____ 30 _____ 2 _____ 95

4. 105 _____ 15 _____ 3 _____ 4

5. 6 _____ 12 _____ 9 _____ 18

6. 16 _____ 19 _____ 18 _____ 17

7. 72 _____ 8 _____ 8 _____ 72

8. 57 _____ 25 _____ 15 _____ 480

9. 50 _____ 20 _____ 6 _____ 5

10. 29 _____ 21 _____ 7 _____ 26

11. 98 _____ 49 _____ 25 _____ 50

12. 106 _____ 2 _____ 4 _____ 53

Writing a Paragraph

A **paragraph** must have a **main idea** and **supporting details**. It should also have a **topic sentence** that tells what the paragraph is about. A good paragraph focuses on the main idea and doesn't stray onto other topics or ideas.

Read the following paragraph. Underline the topic sentence. Cross out any sentences that don't belong.

Tigers are known around the world for their beauty, but they face an uncertain future. Rare albino tigers are white. In the last 100 years, tigers faced both human threats and natural disasters. As a result, they are now one of the world's most endangered animals. By the 1970s, tigers that once thrived in certain areas were gone. You can see tigers in most zoos. Today, India is home to between 3,250 and 4,700 tigers. There are only about 7,000 left in the wild. Humans should try to save tigers. These remaining tigers are threatened by many factors. These factors include human crowding, loss of habitat, illegal hunting, and trade in tiger parts used for medicines.

Now write your own paragraph. You can write about anything that interests you, including a favorite relative, a memory, a sport, a food, a pet, or a hobby. Make sure to include

- a topic sentence
- a main idea
- supporting detail

_____

_____

_____

_____

_____

_____

_____

Mixed Fraction Practice

Add or subtract to solve each problem.

1. Last week, Megan's bean plant was $2\frac{3}{4}$ inches high. This week it grew another $1\frac{5}{6}$ inches. How tall is the bean plant now? _____ $4\frac{7}{12}$ inches _____

2. Jordan ate $\frac{1}{3}$ of the pizza yesterday. His brother ate $\frac{1}{4}$ of the pizza today. If their dad ate another $\frac{1}{4}$, how much of the pizza is left? _____

3. Isel has $\frac{1}{5}$ left from one bottle of glue and $\frac{2}{3}$ left from another bottle. If she poured all the glue into one bottle, how much would she have? _____

4. Kenny sold $\frac{3}{4}$ of his tickets for the raffle. Yasmin sold $\frac{7}{12}$ of her tickets. Barry sold $\frac{4}{6}$ of his tickets. Each child started with 12 tickets. How many tickets did they sell all together? _____

5. Tammy cut the cake into 20 pieces. Skip ate $\frac{1}{10}$ of the cake. Kristin ate $\frac{2}{5}$ of the cake. Caleb ate $\frac{1}{5}$ of the cake. How many pieces of cake are left over?

_____

6. Riley uses $\frac{1}{6}$ tank of gas to drive to work. If he starts with $\frac{8}{12}$ of a tank, how much does he have left when he gets to work? _____

7. $3\frac{1}{3} + 8\frac{9}{12} =$

8. $5\frac{4}{6} - 2\frac{1}{4} =$

9. $7\frac{3}{8} - 6\frac{3}{4} =$

10. $4\frac{1}{8} + 4\frac{3}{16} =$

11. $14\frac{3}{9} - 10\frac{2}{6} =$

12. $3\frac{9}{10} + 7\frac{3}{5} =$

Marvelous Myths

Myths are make-believe stories that explain how things came to be. They usually tell about things that happen in nature. Myths are usually passed down from generation to generation. Read the myth below.

How the Tiger Got Its Stripes

Long ago, tigers used to be bright orange all over. They shone almost as bright as the sun. Then one summer, the sun scorched the earth. Plants shriveled in the heat, and rivers dried up. All the animals of the jungle were looking for shade. The tigers found a perfect place to hide under the cool, spiny leaves of the palm trees. As they rested and played, they didn't realize that the sun burned right through those thin, spiny leaves, leaving black stripes on the beautiful orange fur. And that is why the tiger has stripes.

Choose one of these topics to write a myth of your own. Or, use your own idea.

Why penguins can't fly	How the giraffe got its long neck
How the camel got its hump	Why the moon changes
Why the sun sets	Why the seasons change
Why snakes don't have legs	Why dinosaurs are extinct

Title of Myth: _____

Long ago, _____

_____

_____

_____

_____

_____

_____

_____

_____

And that is why _____

Take a Guess

Probability is a way to guess, or estimate, an answer to a problem.
It can help you come close to an answer without actually solving the problem.

Example: There are 5 marbles in the bag: green, blue, yellow, red, and purple. If you reach into the bag, how likely is it you will get a red marble?

Answer: 1 in 5 or $\frac{1}{5}$

1. How likely is it that the spinner will land on orange? $\frac{1}{8}$

2. How likely is it that the spinner will land on blue? _____

3. How likely is it that the spinner will land on purple or yellow? _____

In this jar of jelly beans…

- 10 are cherry
- 5 are lemon
- 10 are lime
- 3 are grape
- 2 are orange

4. How likely is it that you will grab a grape jelly bean? _____

5. How likely is it that you will grab a cherry or a lime jelly bean? _____

6. How likely is it that you will grab a lemon or an orange candy? _____

7. How likely is it that you will roll an E? _____

8. How likely is it that you will roll an A, a C, or an F? _____

9. How likely is it that you will roll a C or a D in three rolls? _____

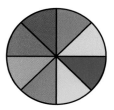

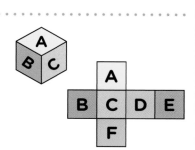

Where Do I Find It?

Circle the reference where you would look to find the following information.

1. The building of the Statue of Liberty

(encyclopedia)   dictionary   glossary   atlas

2. Definitions for words found in the third chapter of a science book

index   table of contents   glossary   almanac

3. Last weekend's hockey scores

phone book   newspaper   atlas   dictionary

4. Record rainfall totals from 1988

atlas   dictionary   encyclopedia   almanac

5. Pages relating to tornadoes

glossary   index   newspaper   phone book

6. Rain forests of South America

dictionary   table of contents   encyclopedia   newspaper

7. This week's weather forecast

newspaper   encyclopedia   dictionary   atlas

8. Chapter about black widow spiders

glossary   table of contents   index   encyclopedia

9. Pages relating to the food pyramid

dictionary   glossary   almanac   index

10. Area codes for your country

encyclopedia   index   phone book   table of contents

11. All home run records set in baseball

atlas   newspaper   almanac   dictionary

12. How many miles it is from your town to the capital city

almanac   encyclopedia   index   atlas

Perfecting Percentages

Follow the directions below.

Solve each problem. Some answers may have decimals.

1. 45% of 100 = __45__   **2.** 15% of 25 = _____   **3.** 50% of 200 = _____

4. 22% of 120 = _____   **5.** 60% of 35 = _____   **6.** 75% of 300 = _____

7. 10% of 168 = _____   **8.** 85% of 536 = _____   **9.** 64% of 80 = _____

Now solve each word problem.

10. Flowers are 25% off at Plant Depot. Tad bought 4 plants originally priced $1.25 each. How much money did he save? _____

11. Price One is having a blowout sale. All merchandise is 40% off! Kang bought 3 T-shirts originally priced $5.00 each and a pair of shoes originally priced $12.50. How much money did she spend? _____

12. Zane's grades are in the top 10% of his class. There are 40 students in all. How many students are in the top 10%? _____

13. Kelli threw 60% of the pitches in last night's softball game. All together, 160 pitches were thrown. How many pitches did Kelli throw? _____

14. Leather jackets are on sale for 30% off. Each jacket costs $96.00. How much did Lisa spend on two jackets? _____

15. Tyra's hourly rate at work has increased 15% per year since she started two years ago. She started at $5.50 per hour. Hint: Figure her last increase was based on the previous year's salary. How much is Tyra making per hour now?

_____

Graphic Organizers

Follow the directions below.

A **graphic organizer** is used for organizing information. It is a diagram in which you can list key words, phrases, and ideas before you begin writing. It helps you organize your main idea and supporting details. Use the main ideas and the supporting details below to complete this graphic organizer.

Main Ideas and Supporting Details

Size of a small cat
Young
Bill like a duck
Furry
Loves to swim

From Australia
Eats worms and shellfish
Hatches from eggs
Drinks milk from mother

Lives in burrows near fresh water
Webbed feet
Flat tail like a beaver
Daily life

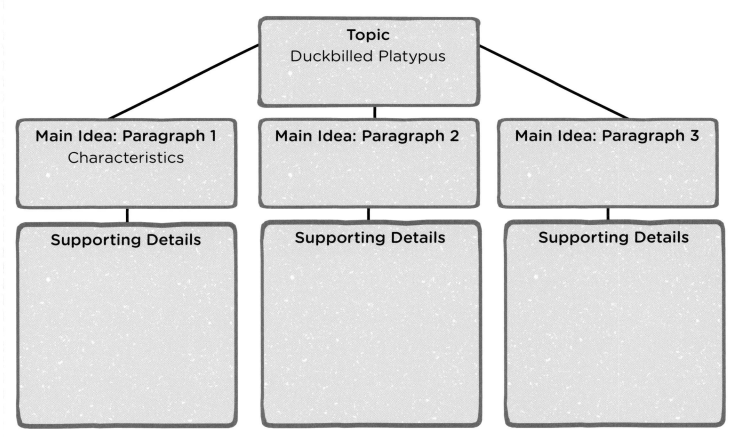

Topic
Duckbilled Platypus

Main Idea: Paragraph 1
Characteristics

Main Idea: Paragraph 2

Main Idea: Paragraph 3

Supporting Details

Supporting Details

Supporting Details

Now, think of a topic you would like to research. Use encyclopedias, the internet, and other resources to find information about the topic. Then arrange the information in a graphic organizer.

Three Cheers for Baseball!

Solve each problem. Some answers may have decimals.

The world-famous Rockets play in
Rocket Baseball Stadium.
The stadium holds 116,000 people.
Section 1 has 12,000 seats that cost $35 each.
Section 2 has 15,400 seats that cost $27 each.
Section 3 has 17,600 seats that cost $20 each.
Section 4 has 23,000 seats that cost $16 each.
Section 5 has 48,000 seats that cost $10 each.

1. The Rockets have sold out the most expensive seats for the last two games. How much did they make in ticket sales for those seats? ___$840,000___

2. Half of the seats in Section 1, 3, and 5 are already sold for Saturday's game. How many seats are left in the stadium? _____

3. Mr. Gant bought baseball tickets for his entire 5th grade class. They sat in Section 4. There are 28 students in his class. How much money did Mr. Gant spend?

_____

4. One night a year, the Rockets sell all the seats for half off. On this night, Jared bought 4 seats in Section 1 and 4 seats in Section 3. How much did he spend? _____

5. The Rockets sold out the entire stadium three games running. How many seats were sold for those three games? _____

6. Rocket Stadium will reduce the cost of the cheapest seats by 20%. If it sells out the entire section for the next 8 home games, how much money will it make? _____

7. Sections 2, 4, and 5 are sold out for tonight's game. Half of the Section 1 seats are sold. All but 1,450 seats are sold in Section 3. How many seats are sold for tonight's game?

_____

8. Each season, Kidz Toys buys 25 seats in each section for its employees. How much money does Kidz Toys spend for these seats? _____

Words in Context

Read the sentences carefully. Which word fits best in the blank?
Use context clues in the sentences to help you choose the correct word.

1. Tonti grabbed a sandwich from the fridge. She hadn't eaten since breakfast and was _____.

a) nauseated
b) ravenous
c) amazed
d) irritated

2. Michael was always at the top of his class. He was _____ and had many goals for his future.

a) impossible
b) unrealistic
c) ambitious
d) puzzling

3. Sofia loved the _____ of the beach in the morning. Only the sounds of seagulls and forming waves washed over her.

a) clamor
b) arrogance
c) serenity
d) turbulence

4. Angry protestors filled the streets. The yelling and shouting increased as the _____ spun out of control.

a) conflict
b) courage
c) harmony
d) disaster

5. Kristin is very quiet and shy. Unlike her outgoing brother, she is quite _____.

a) introverted
b) friendly
c) intelligent
d) disgraceful

6. First he chewed up my shoes, and then he dug up the flower garden. As _____ as he is, he is still a loveable puppy.

a) determined
b) fascinating
c) considerate
d) destructive

7. I can _____ the cold winds and snow. I just don't know if I can deal with the hot summers.

a) remember
b) tolerate
c) surrender
d) suffocate

8. Your speech should _____ people to recycle to help save the environment. Tell them how easy it is just to save water or recycle newspapers.

a) precaution
b) confuse
c) restrain
d) influence

9. Each painting has a _____ style. The colors and the subjects are quite unique.

a) distinct
b) desperate
c) foreign
d) terrific

10. A butterfly's life cycle is one of change. During the pupa stage a caterpillar will _____ into a beautiful butterfly.

a) survive
b) resume
c) launch
d) transform

Using Variables

A **variable** is a letter that represents an unknown number in an equation. To solve a problem with a variable, use one of the four math operations (addition, subtraction, multiplication, division). Use variables to solve these problems.

Example: $12n = 36$

To solve, divide both sides by 12. $\dfrac{12n}{12} = \dfrac{36}{12}$

Answer: $n = 3$

1. An unknown number multiplied by 7 equals 77. What is the number?

$7n = 77$

2. An unknown number multiplied by 9 equals 54. What is the number?

$9n = 54$

3. Brit divided her markers into 10 groups of 4. How many markers did she start with? Write and solve the problem.

4. Darryl has 8 groups of an unknown number that equals 32. What number is in each group? Write and solve the problem.

5. Lily divided her cupcakes into 5 groups of 3. How many cupcakes did she start with? Write and solve the problem.

6. An unknown number of ladybugs plus 48 equals 66. What number of ladybugs is it? Write and solve the problem.

The Benefits of Travel

Drawing a conclusion is forming a thought based on what you already know of the facts and the details in the text. These facts and details should lead you to a logical conclusion. Read the passage below. Then answer the questions.

Traveling is a lot of fun, but it can also be educational. Traveling to different places and meeting new people can teach you a lot about the world. You might see different environments, like deserts, mountains, jungles, or big cities. Each place might be home to different kinds of animals. In Africa you can see elephants and lions. In Australia you can see koalas and kangaroos. In the mountains of North America you can see bears and deer. Visiting new places can also teach you about the people who live there. You might experience different languages, foods, traditions, and clothing. You can visit museums to learn about a place's history and art. Travel is not only an adventure; it is also a learning experience. You will learn to appreciate a whole new world you never knew before!

1. Draw a conclusion about the purpose of this passage.

_____

_____

2. What details support this conclusion?

_____

_____

3. Describe what you think you might learn on a visit to Japan.

_____

_____

4. What details made you draw this conclusion?

_____

_____

5. What do you think would happen if people never traveled?

_____

_____

6. Think of a place in the world you would like to visit. What do you think you might learn during your stay? Write about it below.

_____

_____

_____

Mystery Math Squares

Follow these rules to fill in the missing numbers and solve the math squares.

1. Use the numbers 1 through 9 to complete the equations.
2. Use each number only once.
3. Each row is a math equation. Each column is a math equation.
4. Do multiplication and division before addition and subtraction.

1.

	+		−		**4**
+	■	−	■	+	
	+		+		**16**
+	■	−	■	×	
	−		−		**−3**

19	**−12**	**17**

2.

	+		×		**23**
×	■	×	■	×	
	−		+		**8**
+	■	+	■	+	
	−		−		**−11**

39	**10**	**41**

3.

	+		÷		**9**
×	■	−	■	+	
	−		−		**−11**
−	■	−	■	−	
	×		−		**−3**

9	**−4**	**−1**

4.

	×		−		**4**
−	■	+	■	×	
	−		−		**−9**
×	■	÷	■	+	
	÷		−		**1**

−23	**4**	**38**

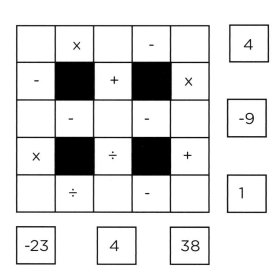

Answer Key

Page 4
Underline: Out, Down, Around, Onto, Into, Off, Over, Into
Poems will vary.

Page 5
2. He tripped and fell down.
3. Ralph forgot his homework.
4. Ralph sat on bubble gum.

Page 6
2. 5,531
3. 1,636
4. 6,025
5. 2,213
6. 6,949
7. 3,791
8. 5,842
9. 6,868
10. 8,555
11. 7,887
12. 3,953
13. 7,851
14. 8,585

Page 7
2. 8,660; circle the 6 in the tens place
3. 17,400; circle 4
4. 93,000; circle 3
5. 212,000; circle the 2 in the thousands place
6. 110,000; circle the 1 in the ten thousands place
7. 25,540; circle 4
8. 860,000; circle 6
9. 66,800; circle 8
10. 19,000; circle 9
11. 500,200; circle 2
12. 680,000; circle 8
13. 35,740; circle 4
14. 71,000; circle 1
A YARD SALE

Page 8
2. neat street
3. fake lake
4. blue shoe
5. smitten kitten
6. glad dad
7. hot spot
8. big pig
9. lazy daisy
10. hairy berry
11. rude mood
12. wet pet
13. small ball
14. cool ghoul
15. legal eagle

Page 9
Answers will vary.

Page 10

Value	🏦💵	💵💵	🪙	🪙	🪙	🪙
$3.52						
$6.23	1	1	0	2	0	3
$4.79	0	4	3	0	0	3
$8.92	1	3	3	1	1	2
$7.03	1	2	0	0	0	3
$5.16	1	0	0	1	1	1
$9.44	1	4	1	1	1	4
$2.65	0	2	2	1	1	0
$8.90	1	3	3	1	1	0
$4.86	0	4	3	1	0	1
$3.99	0	3	3	2	0	4
$9.67	1	4	2	1	1	2

1. $2.73; 2 $1 bills, 2 quarters, 2 dimes, 0 nickels, 3 pennies
2. $2.15; 2 $1 bills, 0 quarters, 1 dime, 1 nickel, 0 pennies

Page 11
2. babies
3. horns
4. boxes
5. men
6. flies
7. mice
8. bands
9. elves
10. watches
11. monkeys
12. cars
13. glasses
14. sheep
15. children

Page 12
Answers to questions 2 and 3 will vary.
4. Leopard: predator; Baboon: prey
5. Giraffe: prey; Lion: predator
6. Lion: predator; Zebra: prey
7. Herbivores: Zebra, Giraffe, Baboon
8. Carnivores: Leopard, Lion

Page 13
2. f
3. e
4. g
5. d
6. h
7. a
8. b

Page 14

1. All rows and columns add up to 14.

11	2	1
3	7	4
0	5	9

2. All rows and columns add up to 16.

10	2	4
1	6	9
5	8	3

3. All rows and columns add up to 20.

10	6	4
8	9	3
2	5	13

4. All rows and columns add up to 23.

14	7	2
6	12	5
3	4	16

5. All rows and columns add up to 32.

12	13	7
17	10	5
3	9	20

6. All rows and columns add up to 45.

10	15	20
13	14	18
22	16	7

Page 15
2. there, they're, their
3. fowl, foul
4. flour, flower
5. marry, merry
6. its, it's
7. so, sew, sow
8. whether, weather
9. wood, would
10. to, too, two
11. do, dew, due
12. heel, heal, he'll

Page 16
2. spear
3. spear
4. horse
5. horse
6. ax
7. ax
8. tree limb

Page 17
1. b) 579,000; c) 580,000; d) 600,000
2. a) 344,800; b) 345,000; c) 340,000; d) 300,000
3. a) 2,488,300; b) 2,488,000; c) 2,490,000; d) 2,500,000

Page 18
2. $14\frac{2}{3}$
3. $9\frac{1}{5}$
4. $17\frac{8}{9}$
5. $4\frac{1}{4}$
6. 6
7. $9\frac{3}{10}$
8. 5
9. $18\frac{1}{3}$
10. $8\frac{1}{2}$
11. >
12. >
13. <
14. =
15. =
16. >

Page 19
1. Wild Willy watched the wavy worms wiggle and wobble.
   ADJ N V A ADJ ADJ N V V
2. Pretty Patty picked a pricey pink dress.
   ADJ N V A ADJ ADJ N
3. Oliver opened the oven to check on oily omelets.
   N V ADJ N V P ADJ N
4. Cheery Charlie chose chunky cheese to chew.
   ADJ N V ADJ N V
5. Harry the hippo helped Hanna hide huge holey hats.
   N N V ADJ ADJ N
6. Funny Frannie found flat flowers under the floor.
   ADJ N V ADJ N P ADJ N
7. Bored Benny bought bundles of bright blue balloons.
   ADJ N V N P ADJ ADJ N
8. Jessica Jones juggled jars of juicy jiggling jelly.
   N N V N P ADJ ADJ N
9. Crazy cats crooned and cried under the moon.
   ADJ N V ADJ N P ADJ N
10. Dizzy Darryl drove his dusty dog in his dirty truck.
   ADJ ADJ N V V N
11. Lumpy, lounging lions laughed and licked lollipops.
   A N P ADJ N V ADJ ADJ N P N
12. A team of tired tigers tasted ten tangy tacos for a treat.

Page 20
1. 5,843; 8,324; 54,388; 58,488
2. 6,279; 69,599; 675,922; 679,299

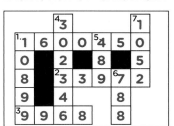

Page 21
1. d
2. e
3. b
4. a
5. h
6. c
7. g
8. f

Page 22
2. early
3. early
4. late
5. late
6. early
7. early
8. late
9. early
10. early

Page 23
2. about 80 feet long and weighs about 12 tons
3. with whistles
4. Yes; Because it's louder than a jet engine and a jet engine is louder than a lion.
5. A baleen whale is a whale that eats by filtering tiny plankton and fish from the water.
6. It gulps mouthfuls of plankton and fish, while its throat expands to form a large pouch. The water is forced through baleen plates hanging from the upper jaw, which catches the food.

Page 24
Summary C
The written summary must include main ideas, not every detail of your summer vacation.

Page 25
1. $1\frac{1}{4}$
2. $4\frac{2}{3}$
3. $4\frac{3}{4}$
4. $\frac{17}{2}$
5. $\frac{7}{3}$
6. $\frac{19}{4}$

Page 26
These numbers are crossed out:
Row 1: 144, 4, 9, 16, 25, 36
Row 2: 81, 49, 1, 100, 121, 64
4 stars are left.

Page 27
Sentences will vary.

Page 28

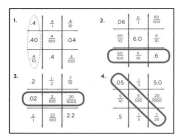

5. $\frac{3}{10}$
6. $\frac{8}{10}$ or $\frac{4}{5}$
7. $\frac{7}{100}$
8. 0.5
9. .06
10. 0.25

Page 29
2. 90.7
3. 26.9
4. 65.94
5. 84.03
6. 40.85
7. 97.15
8. 48.04
9. 23.03
10. 31.83
11. 11.84
12. 20.93

Page 30
2. myth
3. fairy tale
4. mystery
5. science fiction
6. fable
Story descriptions will vary.

Page 31
2. F
3. O
4. O
5. F
6. O
7. F
8. F
9. O
10. F
Facts and opinions will vary.

Page 32
2. 1,410
3. 1,352
4. 144
5. 754
6. 990
7. 3,234
8. 7,304
9. 4,325
10. 5,250
11. 7,684
12. 58,138

Page 33
2. $12
3. 15
4. 20
5. 14
6. 36
A HALF DOLLAR

Page 34
1. milk; shark, share
2. brawl, brake; among
3. speaker, storm, snail; chilly; china
4. pretty; wanted, wasteful
5. engage, enemy; foundation, friendly, fulcrum
6. regal; lawful
7. kingdom, knoll; jelly
8. spread, sprig, spool; dugout, drown
9. parkway, parrot; cloud, clothing

Page 35
IT WAS LOST IN A DAZE

Page 36
Answers will vary.

Page 37
1.
2.
3. cube; drawings will vary.
4. circle; drawings will vary.
5. octagon; drawings will vary.
6. cylinder; drawings will vary.

Page 38
Facts: Humans have only one row of teeth on the top and the bottom. Whenever a shark loses a tooth, a new one moves forward to replace it. A shark goes through thousands of teeth in its lifetime. Sharks use their sharp teeth to catch food, but sometimes they accidentally bite into something that's not food, such as metal! In fact, scientists have found tin cans inside sharks' stomachs. One shark is actually named after its giant teeth. The "Megalodon," which means "big tooth," is an ancient shark that had six-inch teeth. Since the Megalodon lived millions of years ago, we don't know what it looked like.
Opinions: A shark's teeth are its most amazing feature! A shark's mouth is more interesting because it has many rows of teeth. It would be great if human teeth could replace themselves like that! So, people need to be careful not to litter or throw cans in the ocean. With teeth that big, it must have been an awesome sight. It would definitely scare me away!

Page 39
2. calcite
3. feldspar
4. igneous
5. sedimentary
6. metamorphic

Page 40
Answers will vary.

Page 41
1. Scott and Steve
2. Scott started the club because he was worried Steve would spend all his time with Henry.
3. Meetings are held in the tree house. Henry was not able to be in the club because he was afraid of heights. Steve felt guilty about leaving his cousin alone.
4. Steve and Henry
5. Steve started the club because he wanted to do something that Henry could do.
6. Meetings were held on the island. Steve couldn't be in the club because he couldn't swim. He understood what it was like to be left out.
7. Steve, Scott, and Henry
8. Scott started the club because he wanted all three boys to play together.
9. Everyone had fun doing things they can all do together. All three boys played together and had a great summer.

Page 42

		3 + a = b		
a = 4 b = 7 3 + 4 = 7	a = 3 b = 6 3 + 3 = 6	a = 3 b = 9 3 + 3 = 9	a = 5 b = 15 3 + 5 = 15
a = 2 b = 6 3 + 2 = 6	a = 12 b = 15 3 + 12 = 15	a = 10 b = 13 3 + 10 = 13	a = 11 b = 15 3 + 11 = 15
a = 2 b = 1 3 + 2 = 1	a = 8 b = 12 3 + 8 = 12	a = 6 b = 9 3 + 6 = 9	a = 1 b = 4 3 + 1 = 4

2. 1
3. 6
4. 3
5. 10
6. 14
7. 2
8. 13

Page 43
2. 12 students
3. 12 students
4. $\frac{2}{12}$ or $\frac{1}{6}$
5. $\frac{3}{12}$ or $\frac{1}{4}$
6. 24 students
7. hard candy and cake
8. 48 students

Page 44
goat
winter
Christmas
Jewish
Hanukkah
lights
Puebla
American
Thanksgiving
meal
turkey
countries

Page 45

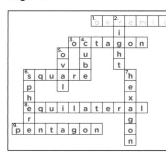

Page 46
Narratives will vary.

Page 47
2. 45
3. 16
4. 24
5. 8
6. 11
7. 20
8. 70

Page 48
1. 72 ÷ 9 = 8
2. 18 ÷ 9 = 2
3. 84 ÷ 7 = 12
4. 56 ÷ 8 = 7 or 56 ÷ 7 = 8
5. 45 ÷ 5 = 9
6. 60 ÷ 10 = 6
7. 21 ÷ 3 = 7
8. 88 ÷ 11 = 8
9. 30 ÷ 5 = 6
10. 132 ÷ 11 = 12
11. 54 ÷ 9 = 6 or 54 ÷ 6 = 9
12. 64 ÷ 8 = 8

Page 49

"Time to get up," Dad called. Maggie and Brett dragged themselves out of the tent. Dad grinned at their sleepy faces.
Brett groaned. "Why do we have to go so early?" he whined.
"Most of the wildlife is out in the morning," Dad explained. "I promise you won't be sorry."
"I'm already sorry," Maggie complained, rubbing the sleep out of her eyes.
After eating a good breakfast, they hit the trail with Dad in the lead. A fine gray mist hung over the mountain. Maggie breathed in the smell of wet leaves, pine trees, and wildflowers. Dad was right. Morning on the mountain was beautiful. Brett wasn't so sure. He dragged his feet and kicked rocks along the trail.
"Would you like to stop up there in that meadow to have a snack?" Dad asked.
"I don't care," Brett grumbled.
"What a grump," Maggie teased.
In the meadow, the hikers sat on a big rock while they snacked on berries, nuts, and raisins.
"Be very quiet," Dad whispered. "We might see something really special." Brett was doubtful. Suddenly Maggie grabbed his arm and pointed to the edge of the forest. A mother deer and her fawn stood silently, watching them. Then the deer slowly walked into the meadow to feed on fresh green grass. Wow, Brett could hardly believe his eyes.
After they left the meadow, Dad turned to Maggie and Brett. "What did you think?" Dad asked with a smile.
"That was amazing," Brett exclaimed. "You were right. This was worth getting up for."

Page 50
Answers will vary.

Page 51
1. >
2. <
3. <
4. =
5. >
6. <
7. <
8. >
9. =
10. >
11. >
12. =
13. =
14. <
15. >
16. >

Page 52
2. Emma and Sam ate eggs and toast for breakfast.
3. Alonzo rides the bus to school each day.
4. I had used the computer to do my research.
5. The lizard runs along the fence.
6. Spring flowers bloomed outside my bedroom window.
7. The earthquake had shaken the jars off the shelf onto the floor.
8. Chloe swims the race with the fastest time.
9. Dad drove us to the mall every Saturday.
10. I had chosen a great big chocolate sundae for dessert.

Page 53
Answers will vary.

Page 54
congruent: b, d
symmetrical: a, c

Page 55
2. 9
3. $5,000
4. 80
5. 240 packs of pencils; 80 notebooks
6. 50
7. 750
8. 126

Page 56

Page 57
2. >
3. <
4. =
6. perpendicular
7. parallel
8. perpendicular

Page 58
2. g
3. d
4. f
5. a
6. b
7. c
8. e

Page 59
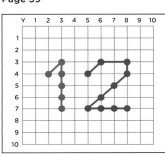
Answer: 12 astronauts have walked on the moon!

Page 60
1. She was sick of the injustice of African Americans having to sit in the backs of buses.
2. African Americans in Montgomery started a bus boycott in protest.
3. It hurt the bus business because African Americans weren't riding the buses anymore.
4. The Montgomery bus boycott brought attention to the civil rights movement. It showed the nation how unfair these laws were for African Americans and eventually helped change the laws.
5. Answers will vary.

Page 61
2. crust
3. mantle
4. pressure
5. magma
6. lava
7. active
8. dormant

Page 62
1. simile
2. metaphor
3. personification
4. Answers will vary.

Page 63
2. congruent
3. not congruent
4. congruent
5. not congruent
6. congruent
7. congruent
8. not congruent.
9.–10. Shapes drawn should be congruent.

Page 64
1. c
2. It doesn't grow like a regular child. It shoots up tall or gets tiny, depending on where the sun is in the sky.
3. Because he sticks close to the child.
4. Any two: He hasn't got a notion of how children ought to play,
And he can only make a fool of me in every sort of way.
But my lazy little shadow, like an arrant sleepy-head
Had stayed at home behind me and was fast asleep in bed.
5. Because he didn't get up with the child and stayed in bed sleeping.

Page 65
a) 6
b) 2
c) 7
d) 1
e) 4
f) 9
g) 3
h) 5
i) 10
j) 8

Page 66
2. 30%
3. 20%
4. 10%
5. Friday
6. Wednesday
7. 5
8. Wednesday to Thursday

Page 67
2. $4.57
3. $4.15
4. $4.88
5. $2.24
6. $3.65
7. $5.70
8. $4.58
9. $7.25
10. $8.22
11. $7.12
12. $10.28

Page 68
Cinquains will vary.

Page 69
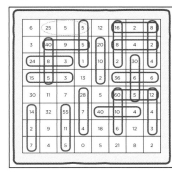
Batter: 1,1
Pitcher: 3,4
1st Base: 8,1
2nd Base: 8,8
3rd Base: 1,8

Page 70
1776; Declaration of Independence
1783; money
1796–1801; John Adams
1803: Louisiana Purchase
1819: Virginia

Page 71
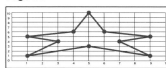

Page 72
Similes and metaphors will vary.

Page 73
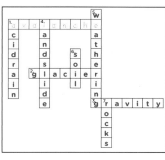

Page 74
2. Setting: hospital
Mood: serious
3. Setting: Sally's room
Mood: hopeful
4. Setting: Mrs. Grady's garden
Mood: happy

Page 75
2. 40,000 + 3,000 + 600 + 0 + 2
3. 700,000 + 90,000 + 4,000 + 800 + 30 + 3
4. 200,000 + 70,000 + 7,000 + 500 + 10 + 8
5. 1,000,000 + 300,000 + 50,000 + 5,000 + 600 + 70 + 4
6. 83,972
7. 51,885
8. 662,093
9. 317,545
10. 2,725,598
11. 7 hundred thousands, 9 ten thousands, 8 thousands, 4 hundreds, 4 tens, 2 ones
12. 6 millions, 9 hundred thousands, 9 ten thousands, 1 thousand, 7 hundreds, 2 tens, 5 ones

Page 76
2. yes
3. yes
4. loves
5. are
6. yes
7. jumps
8. begs
9. yes
10. takes
11. know
12. has
13. yes
14. want
15. likes
16. yes
17. yes
18. falls

Page 77

1) This summer, my dad wanted to fix up our house. 2) He read an article in *Home Improvement* magazine about how to do repairs. 3) We didn't have many tools at our house. 4) My dad has a saw, a hammer, and some nails. 5) We tried to do the repairs, but my dad's tools were too old. 6) We weren't able to fix anything correctly. 7) So I decided it was time to ask for some help. 8) I looked through the Chicago Gazette for an advertisement. 9) I saw an ad for a man named Mr. Fix It, so I wrote him a letter. 10) I asked him to come to 355 Mulberry Street and help us with our repairs. 11) A few days later Mr. Fix It showed up at our house. 12) He knew how to do just about everything. 13) He had all kinds of great tools, so the job was fast and easy. 14) What would we have done without Mr. Fix It? 15) Within a few days, everything was fixed. 16) The only problem was that my dad's old tools were all broken!

Page 78

2. $\frac{3}{6} = \frac{1}{2}$
3. $\frac{4}{16} = \frac{1}{4}$
4. $\frac{3}{12} = \frac{1}{4}$
5. $\frac{6}{9} = \frac{2}{3}$
6. $\frac{4}{8} = \frac{1}{2}$
7. $\frac{15}{15} = 1$
8. $\frac{2}{10} = \frac{1}{5}$
9. $\frac{4}{6} = \frac{2}{3}$
10. $\frac{4}{12} = \frac{1}{3}$

Page 79

2. them
3. She
4. She
5. her
6. their
7. He
8. They
9. She
10. it
11. It
12. them
13. They
14. me
15. It
16. I
17. We
18. our

Page 80

2. 20% = 0.2
3. 15% = 0.15
4. 12% = 0.12
5. 8% = 0.08
6. 4 kids

Page 81

1. Gather the ingredients.
2. Let the pie cool for at least 10 minutes before serving.
3. Grease the bottom of a large pie plate.
4. Test the pie for doneness by inserting a knife in the middle.
5. Yes. Reasons will vary.
6. Instructions will vary.

Page 82

2. B
3. B
4. A
5. A
6. B

Page 83

2. Circle: 10, 4, 5, 2, 1, 20; 6 factors
3. Circle: 7; 1 factor
4. Circle: 6, 9, 4, 12, 3; 5 factors
5. Circle: none; 0 factors
6. Circle: 25, 2, 100, 50, 10, 5, 20; 7 factors
7. Circle: 9, 6, 3, 18; 4 factors
8. Circle: 8, 4; 2 factors
A PROMISE
9. 2, 16, 1
10. 2, 4, 6
11. 7, 4, 2, 1
12. 10, 30, 1, 6, 2

Page 84

Page 85

"Oh no!" said Pam. "We'll never be able to sail without some wind."
"We just need to be patient and wait for the wind," Sam said.
"We can't wait around all day. We need to do something."
"What can we do?" Sam asked.
"We can't control the wind!"
"Let's close our eyes and think about the wind," Pam said. "Think of the windiest day you can remember."
"Okay," Sam said.
Pam shouted, "Hooray! Now we can go sailing."
The wind even blew Pam's copies of the "Sail Away" article from *Sailing* magazine out of the boat.
"Gee, Sam," Pam said. "You didn't have to think that hard!

Page 86

2. 43.0; 186; 5,009; 3.3
3. 16,300; 89; 8,510; 726
4. 39.05; 0.08; 194; 907.6
5. 0.1; 782; 29.2; 8,419
6. 360; 1,390; 100,100; 78,050
7. 1.5; 271.8; 86.61; 9.07
8. 35.5; 722; 8,101; 90.9
9. 545,010; 180; 14; 43,000

Page 87

Movie reviews may vary.

Page 88

These statements are false and crossed out: 2, 7, 8, and 9.

Page 89

Page 90

2. children's
3. Women's
4. babies'
5. rats'
6. girls'
7. horses
8. students'
9. boxes'
10. grandma's
11. puppies'
12. ladies
A CHICK IN AN EGG

Page 91

2. respiratory
3. nervous
4. digestive
5. immune
6. skeletal
7. muscular
8. lymphatic

Page 92

Conflict: Robin wanted to camp by a lake so she could swim. Katie wanted to camp in the desert where she could rock climb.
Resolution: The family camped at the beach where Robin could swim and Katie could rock climb.

Page 93

Olives: cheese, mushrooms, bacon, chicken, onions, egg, broccoli, sprouts
Cheese: mushrooms, bacon, chicken, onions, egg, broccoli, sprouts
Mushrooms: bacon, chicken, onions, egg, broccoli, sprouts
Bacon: chicken, onions, egg, broccoli, sprouts
Chicken: onions, egg, broccoli, sprouts
Onions: egg, broccoli, sprouts
Egg: broccoli, sprouts
Broccoli: sprouts

Page 94

Descriptive adjectives will vary. Sentences will vary.

Page 95

2. Inference
3. Fact
4. Inference
5. Fact
6. Fact
7. Inference
8. Inference
9. Inference
10. Inference

Page 96

1. 14
2. 26
3. -2
4. 10
5. 9
6. 1
7. 3
8. 6
9. 3

Page 97

1. Bold, brave, or adventurous; the family members live adventurous lives.
2. Falling quickly; "He jumped out of windows" and "ten long stories to the ground."
3. Because they might not know what to do, so it's better to have someone with them.
4. Impress or amaze; she sails off the jumps in to the air and the crowd cheers.
5.–6. Sentences will vary.

Page 98

2. -5
3. -6
4. -3 + -6 = -9
5. -4 + -4 = -8
6. -8
7. -9
8. -9
9. -7
10. -11

Page 99

2. a
3. e
4. c
5. b
6. 4, 3, 1, 2, 5

Page 100

2. 225
3. 25
4. Wednesday and Thursday
5. rise
6. 175

Page 101

2. c
3. b
4. d
5. a
6. b
7. c
8. b
9. d
10. a
11. b
12. d

Page 102

Nouns: summer, geyser, presidents, drive
Proper Nouns: Colorado, Reggie, Yellowstone, Mount Rushmore
Verbs: reached, packed, told, took
Verb Phrases: should go, will have, could hardly believe, had bought

Page 103
2. 64 ft.
3. 54 ft.
4. 48 sq. ft.
5. 50 sq. ft.
6. 40 sq. ft.
7. 60 sq. ft.
8. 334 ft.
9. 362 sq. ft.

Page 104
2. length
3. teeth
4. reptile
5. star
6. ocean
7. calves
8. hand
9. river
10. words
11. foot
12. baseball
13. England
14. grandma
15. Japanese
16. jungle
17. children
18. frog

Page 105
Answers will vary.

Page 106
2. Range: 27
Mode: 98
Median: 84
Mean: 87
3. Range: 51
Mode: 36
Median: 79
Mean: 71
4.

Stems	Leaves
3	2 4 6 6
4	2 8
5	0 5
8	1

Range: 49
Mode: 36
Median: 42
Mean: 46
5.

Stems	Leaves
6	2 5 6
7	3 5 9
8	4 7 7

Range: 25
Mode: 87
Median: 75
Mean: 75

Page 107
Aaron: painting
Ellie: swimming
Jake: hiking
Nicole: canoeing

Page 108
Letters will vary.

Page 109
2. feet
3. miles
4. centimeters
5. 12 ounces
6. 200 pounds
7. 3 ounces
8. 2 tons

Page 110
2. $8.80
3. $15.20; $4.80
4. $11.16
5. $9.35
6. $10.65; $4.35
7. $13.05
8. $26.40

Page 111
2. wisdom
3. love
4. understanding
5. wealth
6. freedom
7. joy
8. intelligence
Answers will vary.

Page 112

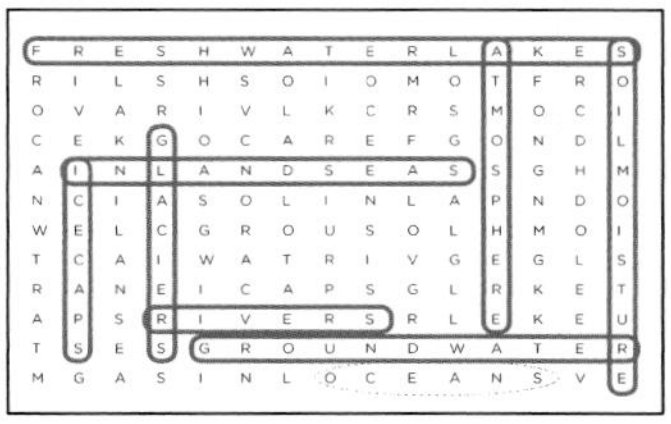

Page 113
2. Baleen
3. plates
4. plankton and krill
5. porpoise
6. killer whale
7. humpback
8. gray

Page 114
2. 24 feet; 288 inches
3. 120 meters; 12,000 centimeters
4. 74 inches; 1.90 meters
5. 36,000 meters; 22.32 miles
6. 19.8 meters; 22 yards

Page 115
Sentences will vary.

Page 116
2. gerund
3. gerund
4. verb
5. gerund
6. verb
7. gerund
8. gerund

Page 117
2. right
3. isosceles
4. scalene
5. isosceles
7. a = 40°
8. c = 155°
9. a = 70°
10. a = 60°

Page 118
1. Cheetahs 33; Mustangs 30
2. 38 yards; 42 yards
3. Cheetah 25 yard line; 50%
4. 151 yards
5. 70 yards; 7 first downs
6. Cheetahs 39; Mustangs 40

Page 119
2. Jaguars and toucans live in the rain forest.
3. Tina, Shiki, and Sonya are talented dancers.
4. Blue whales and dolphins are mammals that live in the ocean.
5. Shells, starfish, and crabs are on the beach.
6. Cats are fun and lovable but can be difficult to train.
7. Cell phones are good for safety but can be annoying to people around you.
8. Red fire ants should be left alone or removed by a professional.
9. Daniel runs very fast but doesn't like football.
10. Trina lives in the mountains and grows all of her own food.

Page 120
2. parallelogram; C = 135°
3. trapezoid; D = 155°
4. rhombus; D = 165°
5. rhombus; B = 60°
6. parallelogram; A = 40°
7. rectangle; A = 90°
8. square; B = 90°

Page 121
Answers will vary.

Page 122
1. surfing the tube
2. language or terms
3. drop in on someone else's wave
4. any three: mullering, donut, eating it, pounding
5. goofy foot
6. happy or excited

Page 123
1. b
2. c
Answers will vary.

Page 124
2. $\frac{6}{8} = \frac{3}{4}$
3. $\frac{2}{2} = 1$
4. $\frac{6}{5} = 1\frac{1}{5}$
5. $\frac{5}{7}$
6. $\frac{5}{8}$
7. $\frac{6}{12} = \frac{1}{2}$
8. $\frac{10}{11}$
9. $\frac{4}{6} = \frac{2}{3}$
10. $\frac{4}{3} = 1\frac{1}{3}$

Page 125
2. 55.05
3. 2.04
4. 9.035
5. 0.0003
6. 0.0085
7. .0127
8. 0.0006
9. 0.0058, 0.058, 0.580, 5.80, 58.0
10. 0.001, 0.10, 1.001, 10.01, 100.10
11. 0.0091, .0910, 9.010, 9.910, 9,001
12. 0.00537, 0.0537, 5.371, 53.07, 537.00

Page 126
2. expository
3. persuasive
4. descriptive
5. expository
6. narrative
7. persuasive
8. descriptive

Page 127
2. $\frac{4}{6}$, $\frac{1}{6}$
3. $\frac{9}{15}$, $\frac{5}{15}$
4. $\frac{4}{8}$, $\frac{6}{8}$
5. 12
6. 18
7. 20
8. 9

Page 128
2. c
3. c
4. a
5. b
6. b
7. c
8. a

Page 129
Persuasive writing will vary.

Page 130
2. The surface is 10,832 degrees Farenheit (6,000 degrees Celsius). The atmosphere is millions of degrees.
3. They are dark spots on the sun that are cooler in temperature.
4. A million Earths would fit inside the sun, and 109 Earths would fit across its diameter.
5. It gives us light, heat, warmth, and energy.

Page 131
1. summer
2. You can be outdoors day and night. Warm weather is great for swimming, hiking, and boating. Vacation from school gives you freedom and fun.
3. winter
4. You can have fun indoors and outdoors. You can ski, snowboard, or sled. Festive holidays bring families together.
5. Answers will vary.

Page 132

Double Chocolate Tower Cake

1 Cake	5 Cakes	8 Cakes
1 cup butter, softened	5 cups	8 cups
1 Tbsp. instant coffee	5 Tbsp.	8 Tbsp.
$1\frac{1}{3}$ cups water	$6\frac{2}{3}$ cups	$10\frac{2}{3}$ cups
8 oz. chocolate chips	40 oz.	64 oz.
5 eggs	25 eggs	40 eggs
2 tsp. vanilla	3 Tbsp., 1 tsp.	5 Tbsp., 1 tsp.
$2\frac{1}{4}$ cups flour	$11\frac{1}{4}$ cups	18 cups
$1\frac{1}{2}$ Tbsp. baking powder	$7\frac{1}{2}$ Tbsp.	12 Tbsp.
$\frac{1}{2}$ tsp. salt	$2\frac{1}{2}$ tsp.	4 tsp.
$1\frac{1}{2}$ tsp. cinnamon	$2\frac{1}{2}$ Tbsp.	4 Tbsp.

Chocolate Fudge Icing

1 Batch	5 Batches	8 Batches
$\frac{3}{4}$ cup heavy cream	$3\frac{3}{4}$ cups	6 cups
6 oz. chocolate chips	30 oz.	48 oz.
$\frac{1}{4}$ tsp. vanilla	$1\frac{1}{4}$ tsp.	2 tsp.
3 cups powdered sugar	15 cups	24 cups
2 Tbsp. milk	10 Tbsp.	16 Tbsp.

Page 133
2. *Mona Lisa*
3. "If I Had a Brontosaurus"
4. Harry Potter and the Chamber of Secrets
5. Legends of the Hidden Temple
6. "America the Beautiful"
7. If I Were in Charge of the World and Other Worries
8. Los Angeles Times
9. Sports Illustrated for Kids
10. "Lost in the Middle of the Night"
11. Romeo and Juliet
12. "How the Tiger Got Its Stripes"
13. "Ten Tricks to Teach Your Dog"
14. "Farmer in the Dell"
15. Julie of the Wolves
16. The Road to Rock and Roll
Sentences will vary.

Page 134
Answers will vary.

Page 135
1. Perimeter: 22 inches
   Area: 28 inches^2
2. Perimeter: 17 cm
   Area: 15 cm^2
3. Perimeter: 12 yards
   Area: 9 yards^2
4. Perimeter: 36 feet
   Area: 54 feet^2
5. Perimeter: 28 inches
   Area: 40 inches^2
6. Perimeter: 18 feet
   Area: 14 feet^2

Page 136
Kevin: beagles
Luke: poodles
Mira: labs
Tham: huskies
Raul: dalmations

Page 137
New words will vary.

Page 138
Answers will vary.

Page 139
2. 24
3. 38
4. 16
5. basketball; soccer
6. 220 students

Page 140
1. Darkness filled my room like a thick blanket. Their trees held onto their leaves like protective mothers.
2. friendly and greeting
3. show her cheery face
4. velvet veil, black
5. screeched and clattered; the branch against the house
6.–8. Sentences will vary.

Page 141
Answers will vary.

Page 142
1. 28 = (7 × 8) − 28
2. 77 − (13 × 3) = 38
3. 80 + (30 ÷ 2) = 95
4. 105 = 15 × (3 + 4)
5. 6 × (12 − 9) = 18
6. 16 + (19 − 18) = 17 or (16 + 19) − 18 = 17
7. (72 ÷ 8) × 8 = 72
8. (57 − 25) × 15 = 480
9. 50 = 20 + (6 × 5) or (50 − 20) ÷ 6 = 5
10. 29 − (21 ÷ 7) = 26
11. (98 ÷ 49) × 25 = 50
12. (106 × 2) ÷ 4 = 53

Page 143
Underline: Tigers are known around the world for their beauty, but they face an uncertain future.
Cross out: Rare albino tigers are white. You can see tigers in most zoos. Humans should try to save tigers.
Paragraphs will vary.

Page 144
2. $\frac{1}{6}$
3. $\frac{13}{15}$
4. 24 tickets
5. 6 pieces
6. $\frac{1}{2}$ tank
7. 12 $\frac{1}{12}$
8. 3 $\frac{5}{12}$
9. $\frac{5}{8}$
10. 8 $\frac{5}{16}$
11. 4
12. 11 $\frac{1}{2}$

Page 145
Myths will vary.

Page 146
2. $\frac{2}{8}$ or $\frac{1}{4}$
3. $\frac{2}{8}$ or $\frac{1}{4}$
4. $\frac{3}{30}$ or $\frac{1}{10}$
5. $\frac{20}{30}$ or $\frac{2}{3}$
6. $\frac{7}{30}$
7. $\frac{1}{6}$
8. $\frac{3}{6}$ or $\frac{1}{2}$
9. $\frac{2}{6}$ or $\frac{1}{3}$

Page 147
2. glossary
3. newspaper
4. almanac
5. index
6. encyclopedia
7. newspaper
8. table of contents
9. index
10. phone book
11. almanac
12. atlas

Page 148
2. 3.75
3. 100
4. 26.4
5. 21
6. 225
7. 16.8
8. 455.6
9. 51.2
10. $1.25
11. $16.50
12. 4 students
13. 96 pitches
14. $134.40
15. $7.27

Page 149

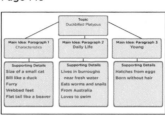

Graphic organizers will vary.

Page 150
2. 77,200 seats
3. $448
4. $110
5. 348,000 seats
6. $3,072,000
7. 108,550 seats
8. $2,700

Page 151
2. c
3. c
4. a
5. a
6. d
7. b
8. d
9. a
10. d

Page 152
1. 11
2. 6
3. 40; n ÷ 4 = 10
4. 4; 8n = 32
5. 15; n ÷ 3 = 5
6. 18; n + 48 = 66

Page 153
1. to persuade people to travel
2. Possible answer: Traveling to different places and meeting new people can teach you a lot about the world. You can learn to appreciate a whole new world you never knew before!
3. Answers will vary.
4. The passage says that in each new place, I might see different animals and people. I might learn about the people who live there, including their history and art.
5. They might not learn to appreciate other countries and cultures.
6. Answers will vary.

Page 154

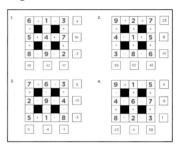

Image Credits

All images by Depositphotos, Dreamstime, iStockphoto, Shutterstock, Thinkstock, and Wikimedia Foundation with the following exceptions:
© AS400 DB/Corbis: 121; © Roger Hill/Science Source: 72; © Massachusetts Historical Society, Boston, MA/Bridgeman Art Library: 53 left; © Museum of Fine Arts, Boston: 53 right; NASA: 59; © Universal History Archive/UIG/Getty Images: 60; © John Warburton-Lee Photography/Alamy: 79 bottom.